CHALCEDON MONOGRAPH SERIES

A CONQUERING FAITH:
DOCTRINAL FOUNDATIONS FOR CHRISTIAN REFORMATION

by

William O. Einwechter

CHALCEDON FOUNDATION
VALLECITO, CALIFORNIA 95251

Printed on acid-free paper

Printed in the United States of America

ISBN 1-891375-20-2

Published by Chalcedon Foundation
P.O. Box 158
Vallecito, CA 95251

CHALCEDON MONOGRAPH SERIES

Other titles in this series:

God's Plan for Victory
Rousas John Rushdoony

The Future of the Conservative Movement
Edited by Andrew Sandlin

The Church as God's Armory
Brian M. Abshire

The Late Great GOP and the Coming Realignment
Colonel V. Doner

The Influence of Historic Christianity on Early America
Archie P. Jones

Contents

Author's Preface

The word "reformation" speaks of change, a change for the better. When a man, institution, or system has defects and faults, or is plagued by abuses and misconduct, we say that there is a need for reformation. Reformation takes place when better policies, procedures, and practices replace those that have failed. But the starting point of reformation is always a change in thinking. Men act in accord with their presuppositions and ideas. Biblically speaking, reformation always begins when men return to the truths revealed in Holy Scripture. Or to state it in a different way, reformation begins with a return to sound doctrine. This is illustrated both in Scripture and in history. The great reformation in the days of Josiah began when the "book of the law of the Lord given by Moses" was found in the Temple. As the law was read to them, the king and people heard the truth of the Word of God and began to act according to its teaching (cf. 2 Chron. 34:14 - 35:27). In the days of Martin Luther, the great doctrines of *sola scriptura*, *sola fide*, and *sola gratia* were rediscovered in the Bible, and the great Protestant Reformation was launched. Then, God gave teachers to His church who, under the guidance of the Holy Spirit and Word, gave to the church a sound theological basis to go forth and transform the Western world, bringing salvation, liberty, and prosperity to men and nations.

But there has been a serious falling away from sound doctrine in our day. The sad results of this defection are all around us. The strength and vigor of Christians and the church displayed during the Reformation and the years that followed have largely dissipated. This is because the robust, God-centered theology of the Reformation has been ignored, forgotten, and replaced by a feeble man-centered theology. The preaching and teaching in much of the church and the perspective in the popular Christian literature of our day sees God as little more than the One who exists to make men happy, fulfill their needs, and affirm their choices. This type of theology has infiltrated, to an alarming degree, into even our evangelical and Reformed churches.

This monograph takes on the particular doctrinal defection of today by providing Christians with an introductory treatment of six vital areas of Christian doctrine. The Biblical teaching concerning God's sovereignty, Christ's lordship in the gospel, the authority of God's law, the self-authenticating truths of God's existence and the inspiration and authority of Scripture, the dominion mandate, and the triumph of Christ and His church in history are necessary antidotes to the man-centered theology plaguing the church at the beginning of the 21st century. If God is sovereign, then man isn't. If the gospel is defined by Christ's lordship, then it isn't defined by man or his choices. If God's law establishes what is right and wrong, then man's reason or feelings do not. If God's existence and the authority of His Word are self-authenticating truths, then we know that there is no neutrality in the sphere of epistemology, and that men must be dealt with as rebels who need a radical conversion and not just as uninformed men who simply need more knowledge. If the earth is the Lord's, then man's duty is not to serve himself, but to bring every aspect of his life into conformity to the will and purpose of God. If Scripture reveals the triumph of Christ and His church in history, then the future must be understood in terms of Christ's mediatorial reign and theocratic plan, and not in terms of either man's utopian or pessimistic views of the future.

Reformation begins with a change in the way men think. A Christ-centered reformation begins when the defective theology of the church is replaced with sound doctrine derived from the Scriptures of the Old and New Testaments. Hopefully, this introductory study will help to change the way we think, and thus provide Christians and the church with some of the doctrinal foundations necessary to effect a Christian reformation of all aspects and spheres of life for the glory of our God and King.

Chapter One

The Sovereignty of God

Although most Christians today would acknowledge the sovereignty of God (though some might do so grudgingly), few have a solid grasp of the meaning of it. This is not surprising given the woeful state of theological knowledge in the church, which, in turn, is due to the absence of theological study and reflection in the church. Many a sermon and writing is devoted to the love of God, the immanence of God, *etc.*, while subjects like the sovereignty of God are sorely neglected. Yet, how unbalanced and detrimental this is, considering the fact that the sovereignty of God is one of the most prominent doctrines of Scriptures, and one of the most important for understanding the nature of God's relation to His creation.

Definition of Sovereignty

Our English word "sovereign" is used both as an adjective and a noun. As an adjective, it describes some person or thing that is above or superior to all others, making them or it supreme in rank, power, or authority. As a noun, it refers to a person or group (*e.g.*, a state) that possess the supreme authority to rule or govern others; hence, a monarch, king, or ruler. Consequently, the idea conveyed by the noun "sovereignty" is that of the status or quality of being a sovereign, *i.e.*, one who has rule and dominion over others due to his position of having supreme authority. The words "sovereign" or "sovereignty" do not appear in the Authorized Version (KJV), but synonymous terms do. Words such as "authority," "power," "dominion," and "rule" translate the

Hebrew and Greek terms that express the notion of sovereignty. For example, the Hebrew root *mlk* expresses the idea of reigning as king (as a *sovereign*), and the related concepts of dominion, rule, kingdom, and kingship. Another Hebrew root, *mshl*, conveys the sense of ruling, lordship, and dominion. In the New Testament, the Greek word *exousia* refers to authority, power, and jurisdiction in relation to the rule of others, as well as to power to do as one pleases and the ability and strength to carry out one's plans and purposes. The idea of sovereignty is found in these and other Biblical terms, and it permeates the Scriptures.

The Meaning of the Sovereignty of God

When Christians speak of the sovereignty of God, they mean His absolute right of dominion over all His creation; that He is the supreme Monarch of heaven and earth because as Almighty God and Creator He is infinitely exalted in rank, power, and authority over *all.* Sovereignty speaks of the divine kingship whereby God exercises His unrestricted power to govern all of His creatures exactly as He sees fit for ends that He alone determines. A. W. Pink expresses the meaning of divine sovereignty in magnificent terms:

> The sovereignty of God! What do we mean by this expression? We mean the supremacy of God, the kingship of God, the Godhood of God. To say that God is sovereign is to declare that God *is* God. To say that God is sovereign is to declare that He is the Most High, doing according to His will in the army of heaven, and among the inhabitants of the earth, so that no one can stay His hand or say unto Him, What doest Thou? (Dan. 4:35). To say that God is sovereign is to declare that He is the Almighty, the Possessor of all power in heaven and earth, so that none can defeat His counsels, thwart His purposes, or resist His will (Ps. 115:3). To say that God is sovereign is to declare that He is "The Governor among the nations" (Ps. 22:28), setting up kingdoms, over throwing empires, and determining the course of dynasties as pleaseth Him best. To say that God is sovereign is to declare that He is the "Only Potentate, the Kings of kings, and Lord of lords" (1 Tim. 6:15). Such is the God of the Bible.[1]
>
> The sovereignty of God in Scripture is absolute, irresistible, and infinite. When we say that God is sovereign, we affirm His right to govern the universe, which He has made for His own glory, just as He pleases. We affirm that *His right* is the right of the Potter over the clay, viz: that He may mould that clay into whatsoever form He chooses. . . . We affirm that He is under no rule or law outside His

[1] A. W. Pink, *The Sovereignty of God* (Edinburgh, [1928] 1961), 20.

> own will and nature, *that God is a law unto Himself*, and that He is under no obligation to give account of His matters to any.[2]

The sovereignty of God, simply stated, is His right to do according to His will, His power to accomplish His will, and His authority to govern His creation as His will determines.

The Basis of the Sovereignty of God

The basis for the doctrine of the sovereignty of God is both theological and textual. *First*, the sovereignty of God is deduced from His attributes. The Scripture teaches that God is independent (self-sufficient and self-contained), meaning that He is the ground of His own being, needing no one or no thing to cause Him, sustain Him, complete Him, or help Him. He is independent in regard to His will and power, exercising both without aid or guidance from any other. In this, God is completely separate from all His creatures because they are by nature ultimately dependent on Him for all things. The contrast between God, the self-sufficient one, and His creatures, the all-dependent ones, establishes Him as the highest Lord and supreme Governor. There can be no criteria above or beyond God that can define or determine Him; no power that can control Him or limit Him; no court that can sit in judgment of Him; no law outside of His own holy nature that can direct or bind Him. God is also infinite in His being—infinite in power, knowledge, wisdom, and holiness. These perfections of His nature establish His right to supremacy in the governing of those who are finite in all respects. As Charnock explains, "God therefore being an incomprehensible ocean of all perfection, and possessing infinitely all those virtues that may lay claim to dominion, hath the first foundation of it in his own nature."[3]

Second, the sovereignty of God is manifest in the doctrine of the divine decree. The word "decree" expresses the Biblical teaching that God has determined by the counsel of His own will a plan that encompasses all His creation, both animate and inanimate. According to Scripture, God's decree governs all things and is single, eternal, unchangeable, unconditional, wise, and all-inclusive. Only one possessing total sovereignty could ordain and bring to pass all events, creatures, destinies, *etc.* But there could be no divine decree such as this if there are competing wills, rights, powers, and dominions in heaven and earth. If Almighty God and His will are not ultimate, then He is not Almighty, and for that matter, neither is He God (perhaps a *god*, but not *God*).

---

[2] *Ibid.*, 22.

[3] Stephen Charnock, *Discourses on the Existence and Attributes of God* (Grand Rapids, [1853] 1979), 2:367.

Third, the works of God determine His sovereignty. God carries out His decree by the works of creation and providence. By creation, the Lord establishes His ownership of all things and His right to govern all things, *i.e.*, His dominion over all. "The sovereignty of God naturally ariseth from the relation of all things to himself as their entire Creator, and their natural and inseparable dependence upon him in regard to their being and well-being."[4] The doctrine of providence teaches that God is actively exercising His authority and power in the creation, and this ensures that the plan of God will come to pass in time and history. Divine providence entails both the preservation of the creation and the government of the creation. Not only are all things dependent on God for their being; they are also dependent on Him for their continued existence. Furthermore, Scripture says that God is the King of all the earth, governing in all the affairs of men so that His counsel will come to pass. Since He is the Creator and the King of kings and Lord of lords, the supreme Potentate of heaven and earth, all must humbly bow to His authority.

The texts of Scripture that teach the doctrine of God's sovereignty are too numerous to list here. May this compilation suffice to reveal the extent of the Biblical witness to this great truth:

> Sovereign Will: . . . *who worketh all things after the counsel of his own will* (Eph. 1:11; cf. Ps. 33:10-11; 115:3; Isa. 14:24-27; 46:10-11; 55:11; Dan. 4:35; Rom. 9:11-19; 11:33-36; Eph. 1:4-5; 3:10-11; 2 Tim. 1:9; Heb. 6:17).
>
> Sovereign Power: *Behold, I am the Lord, the God of all flesh: is there any thing too hard for me?* (Jer. 32:27; cf. Jer. 32:17-19; 27:5; Gen. 17:1; Job 40:1; 42:2; Ps. 89:8-13; 135:6; Isa. 40:12-26; Luke 1:37; Rom. 1:20; 9:19; Rev. 1:8; 4:8).
>
> Sovereign Authority: *For the Lord most high is terrible; he is a great king over all the earth* (Ps. 47:2, 7-8; cf. Ps. 2:4-11; 93:1-2; 103:18; Dan. 4:25-26, 34-35, 37; 7:13-14; Rom. 9:20-21; 13:1; Eph. 1:20-21; Matt. 28:19; 1 Tim. 6:15; Rev. 1:6; 17:14).

The Application of the Sovereignty of God

The doctrine of the sovereignty of God applies to every creature and every sphere of life because this doctrine reveals the relationship of God to His whole creation: His will determines it, His power creates and sustains it, and His authority governs it. All that God is and all that He does is within the context of His own complete sovereignty. The following applications are representative.

---

[4] *Ibid.*, 2:369.

First, the sovereignty of God directs all His works. The works of creation, providence, and redemption are carried out irrespective of the counsel, will, or power of any of His creatures. The universe exists as it does solely because God so willed it. The history of the world has transpired and will continue to unfold in exact conformity to the plan of God for He is present to govern all events and actions of all His creatures. The work of redemption is based solely on the will and power of God. He alone determined the plan of salvation; He alone brought it to pass in Christ; and He alone determined to whom it would be applied and on what terms. God did not consult men on the matter; neither did He surrender any aspect of His sovereignty to men for the accomplishment of redemption. The effecting of man's salvation displays the sovereign power, wisdom, love, mercy, and grace of God.

Second, the sovereignty of God means that His revealed law is the standard of ethics for all men in all spheres. The moral law of God is based on His own perfect nature and is the binding rule of conduct for those that He has made in His image and for His own glory. As law is the will of a sovereign for his subjects, so Biblical law is the will of the Sovereign of heaven and earth for His subjects—all mankind. And since God's sovereignty is comprehensive (He rules over all), so His law is also comprehensive in its reach, governing all spheres, actions, and associations.

Third, the sovereignty of God indicates that all human authority is derivative. Men can only have a measure of authority to govern others if God first grants it to them. There is no *exousia* (authority, power) but of God! The granting of authority to men does not entail the surrender of the least element of divine sovereignty. The delegation of authority is so that men might serve as ministers of God's authority for the sake of His glory and kingdom and for the good of those He has created. Thus, those who rule over men in any sphere (family, church, or state) are under God's law and completely answerable to Him in the use of their authority. Other men are not bound to obey the unlawful commands (*i.e.*, those commands that command what God forbids or that forbid what God commands) of God's subordinates lest they be guilty of disobeying their supreme Sovereign.

Conclusion

The doctrine of the sovereignty of God reveals the glory, power, and dominion of God, and ought to cause all of His creatures to bow to Him in humble adoration and to walk before Him in complete submission. R. J. Rushdoony beautifully states the practical implication of God's sovereignty:

> What does it mean then to believe in sovereignty, government, and providence as a Christian? It means that my life and being are under

the sovereignty and government of the all-wise and most holy Trinity, whose ordering, preserving, and government of all things is for His own purpose and glory, and my only joy and purpose is to acknowledge that sovereign, governing providence, and to rest in its sufficiency. It means that, in every area of life, I must acknowledge and establish rule, law, and authority only in terms of His law word and in faithfulness to His Kingship. This means that, in every area of life and thought, I must assert the crown rights of Christ the King and bring all things into captivity to Him.[5]

[5] Rousas John Rushdoony, *Systematic Theology* (Vallecito, 1994), 211. The quotation is a fitting tribute to the life and work of Rev. Rushdoony. He, perhaps, more than any other in our generation pointed out the usurpation of divine sovereignty by autonomous man. He taught that no man or institution is sovereign, and that only the law of God can serve as a standard for all spheres of life.

Chapter Two

The Lordship of Christ in the Gospel

Soteriology is that division of systematic theology that covers the Biblical teaching in regard to the salvation of men from their sin and the wrath of God. The heart of soteriology is the gospel of Jesus Christ. The gospel is the message of the death, burial, and resurrection of Jesus Christ (1 Cor. 15:3-4), and it is on the basis of faith in the gospel that a sinner is saved from the wrath of God. And as the gospel is the heart of soteriology, so is Christ the heart of the gospel. The gospel is about the person of Christ and the work of Christ to save His people from their sin—it was *His* substitutionary death and resurrection that brought everlasting redemption to them. Now as Christ is the Lord of all things in heaven and earth, and as He is the central figure in God's plan of redemption, it is expedient for us, if we would attain a proper understanding of the Biblical doctrine of soteriology, to approach it from the perspective of the lordship[1] of Jesus Christ.

The Lordship of Christ in Salvation

If men are to be saved from their sin, it can only be in and through the Lord Jesus Christ. The reason for this is that men are in no condition to save

---

[1] In speaking of the lordship of Jesus Christ, we refer to the divine sovereignty He possesses by virtue of His being the Son of God, and by virtue of His obedience and subsequent exaltation as the Christ when He was crowned Lord of all.

themselves. The Scripture paints a dark picture of fallen man's predicament. Man is born in sin (Ps. 51:5; Rom. 5:12), and every aspect of his being has been corrupted by sin, rendering him helpless as to his own salvation. His mind is at enmity with God (Col. 1:21; Rom. 8:7), and cannot understand or receive the things of God (1 Cor. 2:14; Rom. 3:11). His heart is deceitful and desperately wicked (Jer. 17:9; Gen. 6:5). His will is set to do evil, being controlled by the lusts of the flesh and a reprobate mind (Eph. 2:2-3; Rom. 1:28), making him a slave to sin (Jn. 8:34). He has no fear of God, no desire to seek God, and no faith in God (Rom. 3:11-18). What knowledge he does have of God he is actively suppressing (Rom. 1:18-32). The desperateness of man's state is evident in that he considers the gospel, his only hope of salvation, to be foolishness (1 Cor. 1:18). In sum, the Bible declares that the unsaved are dead in their trespasses and sins (Eph. 2:1), and under condemnation (Rom. 6:23). Salvation for such as these must originate in the will of God and be carried out by the power of God.

Most errors in regard to the doctrine of salvation have their roots in an inadequate, unbiblical view of the moral and spiritual status of fallen man. Those who believe that man is merely spiritually sick, also believe that the salvation of sinners is a joint enterprise between God and man. But those who read the Bible accurately understand that man is spiritually dead and can contribute nothing to his own salvation; consequently, they believe that salvation is solely the work of God from beginning to end. To better understand this work of God, let us relate it to Christ, the Son of God.

1. Those who are saved have been given to the Son. During His earthly ministry Jesus made a remarkable statement concerning the salvation of men. He said that the only ones who would believe in Him and be saved would be those who had been given to Him by the Father (Jn. 6:37-40). He also stated that "no man can come unto me, except it were given unto him of my Father" (Jn. 6:65; cf. 6:44). Thus, prior to the incarnation of the Son of God, the Father had determined to give a certain number of mankind to Jesus Christ. Those the Father chose for His Son would also be enabled to come to Christ in faith (cf. Acts 13:48). Who are these individuals that are given to Christ? Simple logic and sound Biblical interpretation indicate that these are those who are called the "elect" in Scripture (*e.g.*, Rom. 8:33; Col. 3:12). Apart from any warrant in the actions of men, and on the basis of His own sovereign will and mercy (Rom. 8:28-30; 9:11-22), God chose who would be part of the blood-bought body of Christ.

The Apostle Paul explains when and on what basis this election of sinners took place: "According as he hath chosen us in him before the foundation of the world that we should be holy and without blame before him. . . ." (Eph. 1:4). The time of the divine choice was before the heavens and the earth were created, and the basis of the divine choice was the work of Christ.

Election was "in him," that is, election is not based on what the elect would do, but solely on what Christ would do for them as their covenant head and representative. To teach that election is due to some kind of foreseen merit in the sinner (such as the sinner's faith) is to rob Christ of the glory due unto Him by making man and his work an essential (though, perhaps, not equal) element in election.

2. Those who are saved are redeemed by the Son. The Son of God came to earth to do the Father's will and secure the redemption of those whom the Father had chosen and given to Him (Jn. 6:37-40; 17:2). Jesus said during His earthly ministry that He had come to give His life for the sheep (those chosen to be part of the fold of God's covenant people) and for none other (Jn. 10:7-29). Jesus did not come to make salvation possible, but to actually procure it for those who had been chosen in Him before the foundation of the world (Eph. 1:7). Jesus' death was substitutionary, that is, He died in the place of those who had been given to Him and thereby took the penalty of the broken law that was due unto them (1 Cor. 15:3; Gal. 3:13). In taking their judgment, He in fact secured their redemption (Col. 1:14), their reconciliation (Col. 1:20-22), their justification (Rom. 5:9), and their forgiveness (Eph. 1:7). Unless they are Universalists,[2] those who teach that Christ died for the sins of all men do not understand the nature of substitutionary atonement, or the efficacy of Christ's blood, which infallibly secures the redemption of all for whom it is shed.[3]

3. Those who are saved are called by the Son. In Matthew 11:25-27, the sovereignty of God in salvation and the place of the Son of God in bringing the elect to the knowledge of the truth is revealed by Jesus. Here we are told that according to God's good pleasure the truth has been hidden from some and revealed to others; and because all things have been delivered to the Son, it is the Son Who reveals the knowledge of God and His truth to those who have been selected to receive it. During His ministry, we see Jesus revealing the truth to His chosen followers, while hiding it from others (Matt. 13:11-17). At the end of His time on earth, He prays to the Father and says that He has "manifested thy name unto the men which thou hast given me out of the

---

[2] Universalists logically conclude that if Christ died for all men, then all men will be saved.

[3] A substitute is one who takes the place of another and performs the duty of another in view of the latter's absence or inability to perform it. There is, necessarily, a one-to-one correspondence between the substitute and the one he is substituting for. A substitutionary atonement means that Christ died in the place of particular individuals (who viewed as a whole are called the elect) who were unable to perform the work of saving themselves, and, consequently, He indeed saved them.

world" (Jn. 17:5), and that He has given them the words of God (Jn. 17:8, 14; cf. 1 Jn. 5:20). Then, Jesus promises His disciples that when He is gone He will send the Spirit of God to teach His people the truth (Jn. 14:16-17; 16:7-15). The exalted Christ is the One Who gives repentance and faith to men (Acts 5:31; 13:48; 16:14), and this He does through His Spirit (1 Cor. 2:11; Rom. 8:11-16). Faith is not, therefore, the sinner's gift to God that enables God to save him, but it is the Son of God's gift to His people (Eph. 2:8) that enables them to lay hold of the gospel and be saved by grace alone.

4. Those who are saved are kept by the Son. Jesus Christ, while on earth, promised that all whom the Father has given Him will be kept by Him (Jn. 10:28-30); not even one will be lost (Jn. 6:39; 17:12). In His high priestly prayer, Jesus asked the Father, Who always hears the Son, to "keep through thine own name those whom thou hast given me" (Jn. 17:11). At His ascension, Jesus was raised to the right hand of God the Father, and from there He exercises a ministry of intercession on behalf of His people. The effect of this ministry is that "he is able to save them to the uttermost that come unto God by him, seeing he ever liveth to make intercession for them" (Heb. 7:25). Paul confidently sees the resurrection of Jesus as ensuring the salvation of the people of God (Rom. 5:10). Therefore, he can triumphantly declare that nothing can separate believers from the love of Christ (Rom. 8:29-39), and that Christ will surely keep those who have committed the salvation of their souls to Him (2 Tim. 1:12). Hence, it is contrary to Scripture and a denial of the power of Christ to preserve His people to teach that a man once saved by the grace of God can fall away and be lost. The Lord enables all true believers to continue in the faith. Any who do turn from their professed faith in Christ thereby give evidence that they were never truly converted in the first place. The true marks of conversion are an abiding faith and a life of obedience to the Word of God. Those whom the Lord justifies, He also sanctifies.

Thus, we see the sovereignty of the Lord Jesus Christ in the salvation of His people! Those who are saved can claim no credit whatsoever, but must rest their salvation in the fact that they have been given to the Son, redeemed by the Son, called by the Son, and kept by the Son. Sovereign election, particular redemption, invincible grace, and faithful preservation can alone account for the salvation of men who are dead in trespasses and sins—men with enslaved wills, corrupt minds, and vile affections.

The Lordship of Christ in Preaching

If the gospel reveals the lordship of Christ, then it follows that any true gospel preaching must exalt the lordship of Christ. Preaching that does not magnify Christ as Lord and call upon sinners to recognize Christ as Lord does not proclaim the gospel in its Biblical fullness and power.

When the Apostles preached the gospel, they did not limit themselves to the historical facts of Jesus' death and resurrection (as important as these are), but were diligent to proclaim the person and attributes of Jesus. In the sermons and speeches in Acts, the Apostles preached that Jesus was the Christ, the Son of God, the Lord seated at the right hand of God, the Holy One, the Prince of Life, the Savior, the Prophet, the Prince, the Judge, and the King. The most prominent appellation given to Christ is that He is the *Lord.* This title sums up His sovereignty and glory as the victorious Son of God Who reigns over all things in heaven and earth. In their preaching, the Apostles called upon men to "Believe in the Lord Jesus Christ" (Acts 16:31; 20:21). Saving faith is, necessarily, connected to Christ Himself and to Who He is.

To preach that Christ died for our sins is not enough; for why should His death save us anymore than the death of some other man? It is the fact that He was the sinless Son of God that makes His death efficacious. The death of Jesus on the cross did not establish the truth of the gospel; it was the *resurrection* that did that because it revealed the person of Jesus and God's acceptance of His sacrificial death. Paul says that Jesus was "declared to be the Son of God with power . . . by the resurrection from the dead" (Rom. 1:3; cf. Acts 13:33), and that the resurrection was proof that justification had been accomplished for His people (Rom. 4:24-25). Peter declares that the resurrection enables men to know that God has made Jesus "both Lord and Christ," and that Jesus now reigns at the right hand of God (Acts 2:30-36). To preach the resurrection of Christ is to preach the lordship of Christ.

Preaching the lordship of Christ in the gospel also requires the declaration of the *finished work* of Christ. Men must be told that the work of salvation is accomplished through the will and power of God alone; that it is Christ, the Son of God, Who redeems the sinner through His vicarious death; and that it is Christ Who reveals the truth to men and gives them repentance and faith. Christ must be exalted and the sinner humbled so that he casts himself utterly on the mercy and grace of God in Jesus Christ.

Finally, preaching the lordship of Christ in the gospel necessitates the calling of men to *repentance.* The essence of man's sin is his claim to autonomy. Man is in rebellion to the authority of God. Consequently, the heart of true repentance is abandonment of autonomy and submission to the authority of God over every aspect of a man's life. To call men to believe in the Lord Jesus Christ is to call them to believe that Jesus is the sovereign Lord of heaven and earth and to submit themselves to His authority; it is to call them to discipleship and obedience—"a calling of the total man and his total life to total service to the Lord wherever he is, and whatever his vocation."[4]

---

[4] Rousas John Rushdoony, *Systematic Theology* (Vallecito, 1994), 530-531.

Chapter Three

The Authority of God's Law

When we speak of authority, we refer to the power or right to give commands, and to require obedience to those commands. A command is the imposition of the will of one person upon another by telling him what he is to do. As Creator, God has complete authority over all His creatures. Thus, He has the power and right to command them and require obedience to His commands. The law of God is the disclosure of the will of God for man that instructs him in how to live and act in a way that is pleasing to God. The law of God is the revelation of the divine imperative for man's conduct and possesses supreme authority.

The Nature of God's Law

What is the essential character of God's law? Is it really *His* law, or is it derived from eternal moral ideals that are ultimate; laws to which God Himself must conform and by which He Himself is judged? In other words, is the moral law part of an independently existing Good that stands over God and man, or is the moral law an expression of the nature and being of God?

The Biblical answer is unmistakable. The Scripture reveals that God is ultimate. As Creator, He is the source of *all things*, both the visible and the invisible. Hence, the moral law that sets the standard for the conduct of man is derived from the moral character of God Himself. God is holy and, therefore, His law is holy. When the Lord commands men to "be ye holy; for I am holy" (Lev. 19:2; 1 Pet. 5:16), He is commanding them to obey His law. Thus, the law is a transcript of His holiness. God made man in His image, and, ethically speaking, man manifests the image of God when he keeps God's law (Eph. 4:24; Col. 3:10). Having taught men to obey God's law (Matt. 5:17-47), Jesus Christ summed up His teaching in the Sermon on the Mount by calling men to emulate the character of God the Father: "Be ye therefore perfect, even as your Father in heaven is perfect" (Matt. 5:48; cf. Eph. 5:1).

The Old Testament term for "law," *torah*, is essential for understanding another aspect of the nature of God's law. When people hear the word "law" today, they usually think of it in narrow judicial terms. However, this is not the primary sense of *torah*. This Hebrew word denotes the ideas of teaching, instruction, giving moral guidance or direction. *Torah* is the means whereby God teaches men their duty and leads them into the pleasant paths of righteousness. The law of God is not legalism, but instruction in living. The law of God is the revelation of God's will so that men might glorify Him and live productive, prosperous lives.

The Revelation of God's Law

God makes His law known to men through both natural[1] and special revelation. God has written the principles of His moral law on the hearts of all men (Rom. 2:14-15). By the divinely bestowed capacities of his mind and conscience, man is able to discern the rudimentary content of God's moral standards for him. This enables man to function as a responsible moral agent and makes him accountable to God for his actions (Rom. 1:20, 32). But natural revelation was never intended to function as the all-sufficient disclosure of God's law. From the very beginning, God has divulged His law to men by special revelation, that is, by His Word (Gen. 1:28-29; 2:16-17). While natural revelation may give to man a general sense of his moral obligations, it is the Word of God that provides the explicit commands to direct this moral consciousness into the path of righteousness. This was true before the Fall; how much more now that man's mind and conscience have been corrupted by sin.

There is no contradiction between the law of God as revealed in nature and that which is revealed in Scripture. But there is a vital difference between these channels of revelation as to their *manner* of revelation and their *specificity* of revelation, and that is what makes the scriptural revelation so superior. As Turretin states:

> The same duties (both toward God and toward our neighbor) prescribed by the moral law [Biblical law] are also contained in the

---

[1]This is often referred to as "general revelation."

> natural law. The difference is with regard to the mode of delivery. In the moral law, these duties are clearly, distinctly, and fully declared; while in the natural law they are obscurely and imperfectly declared both because many intimations have been lost and obliterated by sin
> and because it has been variously corrupted by the vanity and wickedness of men (Rom. 1:20-22).[2]

If men would know the law of God infallibly, then let them look unto the perfect, written revelation of God's law given in the Bible (Ps. 19:7-10).

The Biblical revelation of God's moral law is, therefore, of preeminent authority. However, it is important to remember that the Biblical revelation of God's law is not limited to the body of law contained in such portions of Scripture as the Decalogue, the Sermon on the Mount, or the book of Deuteronomy, but extends to all the Bible. From Genesis to Revelation, in historical narrative and epistles, through prophecy, psalms, and proverbs, God reveals His *torah.* The Ten Commandments summarize the moral law, but the rest of Scripture develops, explains, illustrates, and applies the moral law. *All Scripture* is profitable for instruction in righteousness (2 Tim. 3:16-17).

The Continuity of God's Law

Do the standards of God's moral law vary from time to time or from place to place? Does the New Testament abrogate the moral precepts of the Old Testament and establish new principles for regulating man's conduct? The answer to both of these questions is no. God's moral law remains constant from creation to consummation (and forever after), and governs all men, even to the uttermost parts of the earth. How could it be otherwise?

First, since the law of God is the reflection of the holy nature of the God of creation, it must be universal and unchanging, because God Himself cannot change (Mal. 3:6; James 1:17), and as Creator He rules over all men and nations (Ps. 47:2).

Second, as there is one covenant of grace (the one revealed to Abraham and confirmed by Christ, cf. Gal. 3:7ff.), so there is one covenantal standard of morality. The Old and New Covenants are administrative covenants that govern the application of the terms of one eternal covenant to two separate dispensations. Thus, the differences between the covenants have to do with those matters relating to promise and fulfillment, type and antitype, shadows and reality, not with the essential components of the covenant of grace (*e.g.*, salvation by grace through faith, sanctification by the Word and Spirit). The

---

[2] Francis Turretin, *Institutes of Elenctic Theology*, 3 vols., trans. George M. Giger, ed. James T. Dennison, Jr. (Phillipsburg, 1994), 2:6-7.

Scripture specifically states that the difference between the administration of the Old and New Covenants with regard to God's law will not be the *content* of the moral law, but the *means* employed by God to enable His people to obey it (Jer. 31:31-34).

Third, Jesus and the Apostles confirmed the continuing authority of the Old Testament revelation of God's law for the New Testament church. Jesus emphatically stated to His contemporaries that they must not think that the purpose of His ministry or His teaching was to loosen the authority of the Old Testament law and prophets! No, He had come to confirm and establish the law. Therefore, it was the duty of *His disciples* to do and to teach even the least of the commandments revealed by the Old Testament Scripture (Matt. 5:17-19). The Apostles taught there is one Lawgiver for all of God's people, and that that Lawgiver is Christ (cf. James 4:12; Isa. 33:22; Gen. 49:10). The book of Hebrews shows how there has been a change in the law in regard to the priesthood, the sacrifices for sin, and the Temple because of Christ's superior ministry and sacrifice. But Hebrews never says, or implies, that this change in the law has set aside any of the moral law of the Old Testament. Jesus Christ and His Apostles teach the church to obey the whole counsel of God's law-word (Matt. 22:36-40; Acts 20:27; Rom. 13:8-10; 1 Cor. 7:19; 2 Tim. 3:16-17; Heb. 8:10; James 2:8-12; 1 Jn. 5:2-3).

The Comprehensive Scope of God's Law

As Creator and King over all the earth, the sovereignty of God extends over all creation and over all aspects of man's being and works. Thus, there cannot be any area of man's life that is not governed by the law of God. To limit the authority of God's law to determine the ethical responsibilities for men in any action, association, or domain, is to deny the absoluteness of God's rule over men. And as God's rule is comprehensive, so is the revelation of His law to His subjects. The law revealed in Scripture addresses every area of life: it instructs in personal ethics; it teaches the way of righteousness for the family, church, and state; it gives authoritative guidance for the conduct of education, business, the arts, and the sciences. Berkof states, "The law lays claim, and justly so, on the entire life of man in all its aspects."[3]

God's law is "perfect" and able to keep man from all presumptuous sins (Ps. 19:7, 13), and it is able to instruct man in righteousness so that he will be prepared for *every* good work (2 Tim. 3:16-17). These things could only be said of a comprehensive law that addresses, in precept or in principle, every area of life. And, it is only on the basis of an exhaustive moral law that God could bring every thought, word, and action of men under judgment (Eccl.

[3] L. Berkof, *Systematic Theology* (Grand Rapids, 1941), 614.

12:13-14).

The Proper Use of God's Law

Whenever men speak or focus on the law of God, someone will raise the cry of "legalism." But was David a legalist when he cried, "O how love I thy law!" (Ps. 119:97)? Was Jesus a legalist when He taught men to keep all of God's law, even the least of the commandments (Matt. 5:19; 7:12)? Was Paul a legalist when he said that the law of God was holy, just, and good, and that he delighted in and served God's law (Rom. 7:12, 22, 25)? No! The love of God's law, the teaching of God's law, the use of God's law is not legalism. It is the *wrong use* of God's law that constitutes legalism! Legalism is keeping the law with the wrong motive (Matt. 6:2); it is teaching the law without understanding (1 Tim. 1:7); it is adding human traditions to the law (Matt. 15:1-9); it is seeking justification through the works of the law (Rom. 3:20; Gal. 3:10-11). Paul states that the law is good if one uses it lawfully, that is, uses it as God has prescribed (1 Tim. 1:8).

God has ordained the use of His law in preaching the gospel. The law convicts men of their sin, and drives them to Christ as their sin-bearer and only hope of salvation. The law of God also serves as the standard and guide for sanctification for the believer. The law reveals the sins of the old man, and teaches the new man how to walk in holiness and true righteousness. Additionally, God's law should be employed in society to restrain the wickedness of men, and to serve as the standard of justice that teaches magistrates what sins are civil crimes and what punishment these civil crimes deserve.

The Classifications of God's Law

The common practice of expositors and theologians has been to divide Old Testament law into three compartments: moral, ceremonial, and civil. Although it is true that there is a category of Biblical law that deals with civil matters, this division is a curious phenomenon. Is it not also true that Biblical law speaks specifically to family matters that are distinct from the church and civil realms? Why not, then, add "familial" as a fourth division of the law? Is it because the laws relating to the family are considered moral laws? If so, then are proponents of the three-fold division of the law suggesting that matters of crime and punishment and the exercise of power in the civil sphere are *not* moral issues governed by moral law?

The law of God can be categorized by content (personal, familial, civil, ecclesiastical, etc.), or it can be classified by function (declarative or restorative/ typological). In regard to the latter, Biblical law functions to declare the will of God (man's moral duty), and to set forth the means of restoring sinners to favor with God and of nourishing them in their salvation (God's merciful provision of sacrifice and the sacraments).[4] Using the common terminology, these functions are called moral and ceremonial. This two-fold division of the law is the one that is prominent in Scripture (cf. Ps. 40:6-8; Prov. 21:3; Hos. 6:6; Jer. 7:22-23; Matt. 9:13; 12:7). What then of the division commonly called "civil"? These laws come under the classification of "moral." The civil laws of the Bible are an application of the moral law to the civil sphere. They function as a subset of the moral law, just as the laws pertaining to the family are also a subset of the moral law.

The Interpretation of God's Law

The understanding and application of the righteous standards of God's law requires the use of sound principles of interpretation. First, and most fundamentally, it needs to be recognized that only God can alter, modify, or abolish any of His commandments (Deut. 4:2; 12:32). Therefore, we ought to assume the continuing authority of each and every law of God unless God Himself indicates otherwise in subsequent Scripture. It is presumption for man to set aside any of God's commandments without express authorization to do so from the divine Lawgiver. Thus, the laws of the Old Testament should be considered binding today if they are not abrogated or altered by the New Testament Scriptures (as, for example, the ceremonial—restorative/typological—laws of the Old Testament). This principle of interpretation is based on the understanding that the Bible is its own best interpreter.

Second, each law should be examined according to the pattern of grammatical-historical exegesis. This method requires a careful consideration of the words of the Biblical text in their theological and historical context, so that the meaning intended by the original author can be ascertained. Third, the abiding theological truth and/or moral principle that informs (underlies) the Biblical text needs to be discerned. This is essential, because it is not necessarily the precise cultural or historical expression of the law that is authoritative, but, rather, it is the abiding theological or moral principle that forms the basis for the law that carries over to all cultures and times.

The Challenge to God's Law

The challenge to the truth and authority of God's law began in the Garden of Eden when man succumbed to Satan's temptation to set aside God's commandment and determine good and evil for himself (Gen. 3:5). This assertion of the moral prerogative to decide for oneself what is good and evil

---

[4]Greg L. Bahnsen, *No Other Standard* (Tyler, TX, 1991), 93-94.

is best described as "autonomy." The word "autonomy" means "self-law," that is, man being a law unto himself. Autonomous man claims the right to govern himself according to the moral standards that *he* sees fit to establish. This rebellious claim is based on the belief that man's own independent reason is the final authority for interpreting the moral sphere of life. Autonomy is, essentially, every man doing that which is right in his own eyes (Judg. 17:6). Human autonomy expresses itself through natural law ethics, false religions, human traditions, vain philosophies, and the deceptive teaching of antinomianism.[5]

In the end, there are only two alternatives for determining good and evil: God's law or man as a law unto himself. What choice will you make? Hear the word of the Lord:

> Let us hear the conclusion of the whole matter: Fear God, and keep his commandments: for this is the whole duty of man. For God shall bring every work into judgment, with every secret thing, whether it be good, or whether it be evil (Eccl. 12:13-14).

---

[5]The word "antinomian" means "against the law," and refers to the treasonous doctrine that grace releases the Christian from the obligation to keep God's law. But as Rushdoony states: "Lawless Christianity is a contradiction in terms: it is anti-Christian. The purpose of grace is not to set aside the law but to fulfil the law and enable man to keep the law. If the law was so serious in the sight of God that it would require the death of Jesus Christ, the only-begotten Son of God to make atonement for man's sin, it seems strange for God to then proceed to abandon the law!" *The Institutes of Biblical Law* (1973), 4.

Chapter Four

How Do We Know God Is Real and the Bible Is True?

The question of "How do we know?" is a question that does not cross our minds very often (unless you are a philosopher!); yet, it is a very important question.[1] In approaching the question, it needs to be understood that each of us has developed a particular view about the nature of reality that is based upon an ultimate standard of interpretation. That is, each person interprets (gives meaning to) the "facts" of the world by an appeal to that which he or she believes to be the ultimate criterion for determining reality. This process of judging the facts, takes place, we might say, automatically, so it is not usually something of which we are conscious.

On the basis of a standard, we all interpret the data that comes to us individually and categorize it as right or wrong, good or bad, true or false, helpful or unhelpful, desirable or undesirable, *etc*. This is what is meant when we say that we *interpret* the "facts" of our experience. The resulting interpretation of the particulars we encounter is what we call knowledge. We *know* that something is what we believe it to be because our ultimate standard for determining knowledge tells us that it is so. Therefore, all of our presumed knowledge is actually based upon that which we *presuppose* as the final arbiter of reality. This presupposition, or first-principle, is our supreme faith-commitment; that is, we *believe* that our chosen standard is the best and most

[1] The question of, "How do we know," belongs to the field of study that is called "epistemology." Epistemology concerns itself with the investigation of the origin, nature, and methods of knowledge.

reliable one.[2] This presupposition is the starting point of all of our thinking and the basis for all our predication—of all our affirmations as to the quality, nature, or attributes of the thing (fact).[3] So even though most of us have not given a lot of thought to this matter of an ultimate standard of interpretation, we all have one. And we all, consciously or unconsciously, interpret all the particulars we experience from the basis of an all-controlling presupposition.

That our starting point, our basic presupposition is all-important is evident: if it is sound, our interpretation will be sound; if it is false, our interpretation of the facts will be defective. The goal, therefore, is to have the right presupposition. But what is the right presupposition; what is the proper standard of interpretation; what is the unfailing faith-commitment that will lead us to true knowledge? Men have different answers to this question. For example, the rationalist says that human reason is the standard. The empiricist says that it is sensory experience. The hedonist says that is pleasure. The pragmatist says that it is the thing that works. The irrationalist says there is no ultimate standard because all is pure chance, pure contingency. The religionist says that it is his religion. The Christian says that it is the God of the Bible. In the midst of all this babble, how does the Christian *know* that God is real and the Bible is true, and that, therefore, all other presuppositions are false?

Authority

In the quest for the right first-principle of knowledge, the matter of authority is an inescapable concept. Who has the authority to determine the nature of reality? Who has the warrant to say, "This is the first-principle of knowledge"? When you get down to it, there are really only two possible sources of authority, two possible standards in the sphere of epistemology:

---

[2] We could call this a "faith-commitment" because it is something we accept without any proof beyond the presupposition itself. In other words, there is nothing beyond our chosen standard that we can appeal to to establish it. For example, if we look to reason as the ultimate standard, we do so because it alone appears reasonable to us. If we sought to prove that reason was the true standard by an appeal to sensory experience, then what we have done is set up experience as our ultimate standard because it is used as the basis for our predication concerning reason.

[3] However, men often act and believe in a way that is inconsistent with their basic presuppositions. This is due to the fact that man is a complex being with many factors influencing his mind and his decisions. In spite of this, it is still true that a man will ultimately rely on his chosen standard of knowledge to interpret the facts of his experience. To be aware of one's presupposition and to act in accord with it on a consistent basis is to be an "epistemologically self-conscious" individual.

God or man. Either God is ultimate, or man is ultimate. You either begin with the transcendence of God as Creator and His absolute right to determine the meaning for all facts and the standards for all conduct, or you begin with autonomous man and his categorical right to define meaning and establish standards of action that suit him. Either God is the judge and interpreter of reality, or man is the judge and interpreter of reality.

This leads to a second factor. If man is the authority, then the instrumentality for interpretation is his own mind and intellect—his own reason. But if God is the authority, then the means for interpretation must be revelation; that is, God must make His mind known to man in some understandable and verifiable way so that man can think God's thoughts after Him and interpret the facts of the universe in accord with God's sovereign will and purpose. The orthodox Christian is not in doubt as to *Who* is the authority and *what* is the instrumentality of interpretation. The Christian believes in Almighty God as the Creator of all things and the Sovereign Determiner of all facts, and that the Bible is the revelation of God to man (it is the *Word of God*) so that man might understand God's creation, man's place in it, and the nature and meaning of all things.

Authentication

The fact of the existence and authority of God and the fact of the Bible as the infallible Word of God are, by the nature of case, "self-authenticating" truths. What does this mean? It means that the truth concerning the attributes and existence of God is so great, so fundamental, and so certain that it cannot be proved by reference to anything else. If God is ultimate, then there is nothing that can be employed to verify Him; if there were, that thing would be more ultimate than God for He would have to be defined in reference to it. God has declared Himself as "I AM THAT I AM" (Ex. 3:14). He is the eternally self-existent, self-contained, self-sufficient, self-revealing One Who is faithful to His covenant. He is the sovereign Creator Who made all things, decreed all things, and defined all things, but Who in Himself is determined by no one or no thing. Therefore, God does not seek to prove His existence to men. His existence is the very ground for the existence of man and of the creation. In history and in the Scripture that records that history, God presents Himself to man as *God* in all His splendor and glory, and as nothing else or nothing less.

The Bible is also, of necessity, self-authenticating. As the Word of God, it is ultimate in its authority. It cannot appeal to the word (judgment) of any other to verify its nature without denying its own nature. For example, if the word of man is necessary to establish the Bible as the Word of God, then man's word is the ultimate authority; if experience is required to establish it, then experience is supreme, *etc.* As the Word of the Creator, it alone is infallible in its interpretation of man and of the creation.

Acceptance

If the existence of God and the nature of the Bible as the infallible Word of God are self-authenticating truths, then why do not all men embrace these truths? The answer is twofold.

First, man is in ethical rebellion against God. This means that he *knows* that God is his Creator and that the Bible is the Word of God, but that he revolts against these truths. As a creature, man knows that God exists; but as a sinner, consumed with his own importance, his own desires, his own autonomy, he hates God and the intrusion that God represents to his plans. So, he actively suppresses his knowledge of God so that he can pursue his own agenda (Rom. 1:18-21). Man does not perish for a lack of knowledge about God—man's own being and all creation clearly testifies of God's glory, power, and Godhead (Rom. 1:19-20; Ps. 19:1-6)—he perishes because he sins against the knowledge that he does have. This rebellion began in the Garden of Eden when Eve chose to establish herself, her own reason, as the ultimate reference point of predication (initially, concerning the tree of the knowledge of good and evil), and thus claimed her own autonomy. Eve knew of God and of His interpretive word, but did not believe that God could be ultimate; so, she reinterpreted the nature of God to suit her own autonomy (made God into a god of her own imagination, cf. Rom. 1:23, 25).

This is what men are about today. As Eve, they establish themselves, some other man, or some other aspect of the creation as their ultimate reference point for determining knowledge; they interpret the facts of their experience on the basis of their chosen presuppositions. Then, if they wish to retain the concept of God (a concept that man finds hard to part with), they fashion a god of their own liking (or accept one already fashioned by other men) that is far different than the sovereign, self-contained God revealed in Scripture.[4] It must be so, if they will have a god, because their presuppositions, chosen as they are in the pursuit of rebellion, deny the existence of the Creator/God of Scripture.[5]

---

[4]This is the origin of the many religions of the world (except, of course, Biblical Christianity). These religions are the creations of men (with assistance from Satan and his demons) for the purpose of retaining the concept of God while conveniently denying His eternal power and Godhead.

[5]This analysis does not intend to convey that all men consciously and with deliberation follow these steps. Culture, parental sins, and the like determine the rebellious presuppositions of many. Men do not always have to plot their steps in a definitive way because other sinners have already done it for them; being in the same ethical rebellion, they follow in the paths of their predecessors.

Second, those who do believe in the existence of God and the divine inspiration and infallibility of the Bible do so, not because of some set of rational or sensory proofs, but because of the grace of God that has changed them from rebels to worshippers. When the Spirit of God regenerates a man, that man's epistemology is radically changed: he casts off his own autonomy, buries his false presuppositions, and embraces God as He is and the Word of God as the only true interpretation of his condition and its solution. This being done, the erstwhile rebel now submits to God's authority and puts his faith in the gospel. In salvation, a man comes to embrace God and His Word as ultimate. In sanctification, this first-principle, this absolute presupposition works itself out in the life of the believer as he learns to interpret all facts and all areas of life according to God's Word.

We Christians know that God exists and the that the Bible is true "by the inward work of the Holy Spirit bearing witness by and with the Word in our hearts."[6] This witness enables us to reorient all of our thinking so that now, with our self-imposed, alien presuppositions removed, we are able to see that all creation shouts of the glory of God. We learn that our unbelief was never a problem of the lack of evidence (it is *everywhere*), but due to eyes that had willfully been blinded by false presuppositions derived from a rebellious heart that said, "I will determine truth and falsehood and good and evil for myself."

Apologetics

What, then, is the nature of apologetics? "Apologetics," as a theological discipline, refers to the defense of the Christian Faith against the attacks of all forms of unbelief. Apologetics gives a Biblical defense of the reason for the hope that is within us (1 Pet. 3:15). But, in terms of our encounter with an unbelieving world, what is the purpose of this defense?

Many Christians believe that the goal of apologetics is to open minds and hearts to the truth of God by showing unbelievers through rational proofs and logical argumentation that the Bible is trustworthy and that Christ is the Savior. But this is not the purpose of apologetics. The purpose of apologetics, as Greg Bahnsen has well stated, is not to open hearts but to close mouths. That is, we show the unbeliever the foolishness of his own worldview—that by rejecting the sovereign Creator/God of the Bible he has no basis for meaning, rationality, or prediction, no answer to the question of the one and the many, no hope for the future; and that since all unbelieving thought is bankrupt, he can only live his life by stealing from the worldview of the Christian—then, having shut his mouth, we present to him the claims of Christ without compromise. Only God can open the heart of man to receive the testimony of

---

[6] Westminster Confession of Faith, I, 5.

Christ, and the instrumentality He has chosen to accomplish this is His Word and Spirit.

Since man is a rebel who is willfully suppressing the knowledge of God that is in him and around him, we know that the problem for any particular man is not a lack of evidence for God. Man's problem is sin. He has set himself up as ultimate. Using the Word of God, we must convict him of his sin and show him the redemption that is in Christ Jesus. If the sinner raises objections, we should patiently answer those objections. But in our answers we must never give the unbeliever the idea that he has the right to sit in judgment of God's truth, or that he is the ultimate judge of what the Scriptures say. We must not appeal to his reason as if *that* determines the matter. We, as faithful ambassadors, must deliver the Word of our sovereign God *as* the Word of a sovereign God Who sits in judgment of all men and commands all men everywhere to repent (cf. Acts 16:22-31). We must trust in the self-authenticating Christ of Scripture to work His sovereign will for the glory of His own name.

Chapter Five

The Earth Is the Lord's

As the stubborn Pharaoh of Egypt suffered with his people through the terrible plague of thunder and hail, he called for Moses and Aaron and begged them to entreat the Lord (Yahweh) that the plague would cease. Moses responded by saying that he would go out of the city and pray to the Lord "and the thunder shall cease, neither shall there be any more hail; that thou mayest know how that the earth is the Lord's" (Ex. 9:29). The proud Pharaoh of Egypt had refused to believe that all things in heaven and earth were the property of Yahweh and subject to His rule; but Pharaoh was receiving a first-hand display that Yahweh was indeed Lord of *all.* Later, as Israel stood poised to enter the Promised Land, Moses taught the people the fact of their election by God. This election is all the more awesome to contemplate when Israel remembers that Yahweh is no mere tribal deity, nor one god among many, but the Creator of heaven and earth. Moses states, "Behold, the heaven and the heaven of the heavens is the Lord's thy God, the earth also, with all that therein is" (Deut. 10:14). David stated the truth that God is Master and Owner of all things when he wrote, "The earth is the Lord's, and the fulness thereof; the world, and they that dwell therein" (Ps. 24:1). According to these words, the whole earth belongs to God, including all its elements and all the people who dwell therein.

An important scriptural term to designate God's comprehensive ownership and rule of the world is the term "dominion" (cf. Job 25:2; Ps. 103:22; 145:13; Dan. 4:3, 34). As Creator, God has dominion over all—the entire world belongs to Him and is under His jurisdiction and command.

Significantly, the word "dominion" is used by God to describe man's place and calling in the world (Gen. 1:26-28; Ps. 8:6). It is imperative that the modern church understand the dominion calling of covenant men and women, and the purpose of this chapter is to give a brief introduction to this calling.

Man, the Image of God, and Dominion

Genesis 1:26 is one of the most important verses in all of Scripture concerning the being and calling of man. In this verse, the divine counsel concerning the creation of man is stated: "And God said, Let us make man in our image, after our likeness: and let them have dominion over the fish of the sea, and over the fowl of the air, and over the cattle, and over all the earth, and over every creeping thing that creepeth upon the earth." There has been much discussion concerning the precise definition of the image of God in man, but the general agreement is that it refers to the fact that man will be comparable to his Maker in certain aspects of his being and his work—the Creator Himself will serve as the pattern from which man will be contrived. In regard to his being, man will have a moral and spiritual likeness to God (*i.e.*, he will be a rational being, a self-conscious person, able to exercise a will in moral choices; and a pure being, untainted by sin). In regard to his work, man will, like God, possess authority and power to rule the earth and its creatures (*i.e.*, have dominion). These two aspects—man's being and work—encapsulate the image of God in man. The two are intimately related: man is able to exercise dominion in the earth because he is a rational, self-conscious, and righteous man; and, the dominion responsibility provides the province for the exercise of man's moral and spiritual powers.

It is God's purpose that man serve as His representative in the earth. To adequately fulfill this calling, man is made in God's image. God has endowed man with the faculties needed, the authority required, and the materials and creatures requisite to show forth the glory of God and to provide for his life on earth.

The Charge to Take Dominion

From the beginning it was God's will that man would have dominion in the earth. This dominion is part of the image of God in man. The charge to take dominion in Genesis 1:28 is preceded by the grant of dominion in Genesis 1:26, "and let them have dominion. . . ." The Hebrew word that is translated "dominion" here means to subdue, rule over, or have the mastery of. It can also carry the meaning of, to possess oneself of, or take possession of. According to the context of Genesis 1, it appears that both connotations of the word "dominion" are represented here. In this grant of dominion, God gives the earth and all that is in it to man as his possession and also gives him the authority to rule it. Because God's dominion must remain absolute, man's dominion is one of stewardship. The authority man exercises over the earth has been delegated to him by God, and the assets that man holds are ultimately the property of God. Man, as God's steward and representative, is to use his authority and possessions for the glory of his Lord and Master.

The charge to take dominion in the earth is stated in Genesis 1:28. Here God commands the man and woman "to have dominion over" the earth and all living creatures. The command reflects the grant of dominion, but reveals the fact that man must actively *take dominion*; that is, his work is to take possession of all the earth and exercise a hands-on rule of the earth and its creatures. The necessary steps to fulfill the dominion mandate are stated as: "Be fruitful, and multiply, and replenish the earth, and subdue it. . . ." The work of dominion requires man to be fruitful (*i.e.*, have many children)[1] and fill the earth with people, and for man to "subdue" the earth. The word "subdue" indicates that man must bring all space and resources of the earth under his control.

The dominion commandment instructs man to develop all the riches of the earth so that the full potential of the creation can be realized to the glory of God and the good of mankind. The dominion mandate is comprehensive, calling man to rule the entire world, its creatures, and all aspects of life in accord with the will and purpose of God. David states it this way: "Thou madest him [man] to have dominion over the works of thy hands; thou hast put all things under his feet. . . ." (Ps. 8:6).

The Corruption of Dominion

Man's fall into sin radically changed him. He remained a rational being, but because he had established his own mind as the standard of truth, he would no longer think God's thoughts after Him, so his ability to reason was corrupted. He remained a self-conscious person, but because he did not derive the concept of his personality from the fact of his creation in the image of God, his self-consciousness was perverted into selfishness and self-aggrandizement. He retained the power to will, but lost the ability to choose righteousness, and thus became a slave to sin. But not only was his being corrupted, so was his capacity for dominion. Man's original endowments enabled him to serve as God's representative and exercise dominion in the earth, but when these endowments were depraved through sin, man could no longer carry out his calling. But his *ability* for dominion was not the only

[1] For a discussion of this aspect of the dominion charge as it applies today, see William O. Einwechter, "Children and the Dominion Mandate, Parts 1 and 2" *Chalcedon Report*, 400 and 401 (November and December 1998).

thing he lost, he also forfeited his *authority.* By rejecting God's rule, man came under the rule of sin and Satan—he became a slave, and slaves do not exercise dominion. Only a righteous man operating in the liberty of obedience to God can carry out the charge of taking dominion.

There is a widespread misconception that unregenerate man can still fulfill the dominion mandate. This perspective is based on the view that the dominion calling of man is essentially agricultural and technical. But it is not. The dominion calling is inherently *ethical*, *i.e.*, it calls man to rule the earth and develop it resources as *God's representative* for the honor and glory of his Creator. Man is charged with the task of governing the earth according to the ethical standards of God's law as summarized in the two great commandments of the law: love of God and love of one's neighbor. Unregenerate man does not carry out any of his activities out of a love for God and almost never out of a true love for other men. To some degree, unsaved man still retains the image of God in his person and also an impulse to take dominion, but his focus is limited to the technological, and his motive is his own power and glory. How can it be a fulfillment of the dominion mandate when a man uses his gifts and resources in the context of rebellion against God? The dominion charge is to build the kingdom of God on earth! It is true, that in a limited, physical sense, the unregenerate may contribute procreationally to the filling of the earth and technologically, agriculturally, or scientifically to the subduing of the earth—God uses even the wrath of man to praise Him and serve His purposes. These contributions of the wicked are part of the wealth that is laid up for the righteous (cf. Prov. 13:22; Eccl. 2:26). But only righteous men can fulfill the dominion calling, and that is why in the Bible the charge to take dominion is specifically addressed to men who are in covenant with God.

The Restoration of Dominion

After the fall, wherein man lost his ability and authority for dominion, God in mercy intervened with His Promise (Gen. 3:15). The promise that the seed of the woman would crush the head of the serpent provided hope for man that what he had lost would one day be restored through one of his descendents. This promise also provided the objective basis for man's faith in God and His saving grace. From the beginning, the Scripture differentiates between the chosen line of the seed of the woman and the reprobate line of the seed of the serpent. The line of the seed of the woman originates in Adam's son, Seth, continues in Noah and Shem, and leads to Abraham, the father of all who believe. The promise of Genesis 3:15 is greatly expanded in God's promises to Abraham and his seed (Gen. 12:2-3; 17:4-8), and it is revealed that through Abraham all the nations of the earth will be blessed (Gen. 12:3; 22:18; 26:4), and that his seed shall take dominion in the earth (Gen. 22:17;

28:14). These promises are secured by the covenant that God makes with Abraham (Gen. 15). Therefore, the Old Testament shows that God's covenant with Abraham will be the means of restoring righteousness *and* dominion to fallen man.

The New Testament explicitly teaches that the promises to Abraham are fulfilled in Jesus Christ (Gal. 3:6-9, 16-18, 26-29). He is the second Adam Who restores what the first Adam lost (Rom. 5:17-19; 1 Cor. 15:22); He is the seed of the woman Who crushes the head of the serpent (Rev. 12:1-9); He is the man Who reestablishes dominion for mankind (Heb. 2:6-8); He is the Lord Who is given authority to rule all the nations of the earth (Acts 2:33-36; Rev. 19:16). In Christ, men have their ability to exercise dominion restored (Eph. 4:24), and their authority to rule reinstated (Rev. 2:26-27). Christ is the head of a new humanity (2 Cor. 5:17) that will bring the blessings of the kingdom of God to earth as He leads them in the fulfillment of the original dominion mandate. Through Christ and His seed the task of dominion will be realized when, in time and history, "the earth shall be filled with the knowledge of the Lord, as the waters cover the sea" (Isa. 11:9).

The Means of Dominion

But how is the dominion charge carried out in the post-fall world where it is not simply a matter of subduing the earth, but also of subduing sin and rebellion against God? The answer is found in the Great Commission.[2] The Great Commission should be understood as a restatement of the original dominion charge for the post-fall, post-resurrection of Christ era. The Great Commission as recorded in Matthew 28:18-20 states that the followers of Jesus have the ability ("I am with you," *i.e.*, through the Holy Spirit that I will send to you [cf. Acts 1:4-8]), and the authority ("All power is given unto me in heaven and earth. Go ye therefore. . . .") to go forth as God's representatives to conquer sin and subdue the earth for the glory of God. The Great Commission as stated in the Gospels is reminiscent of the commands of the original dominion charge in Genesis 1:28. Jesus' followers are to preach the gospel and gain converts (*i.e.*, be fruitful and multiply); they are to go into all nations (*i.e.*, fill the earth); and they are to disciple all nations in obedience to the commands of Christ (*i.e.*, subdue the earth).

The Great Commission teaches that God's purpose for man as revealed in the dominion mandate will come to pass as the church of Jesus Christ disciples the nations by preaching the gospel, baptizing the converts, and teaching them to observe the whole counsel of God as it is revealed in the

---

[2] For an excellent study of the Great Commission, see Kenneth L. Gentry, Jr., *The Greatness of the Great Commission* (Tyler, 1990).

Scriptures of the Old and New Testaments. Thus, the Great Commission is not simply a matter of evangelism and church planting, but aims at the transformation of every institution and every sphere of life by the Word of God, and at the development of godly, Christ-honoring culture in every land. The call to Christians is to cast down the foolish imaginations of men, and every thing that exalts itself against the knowledge of God, and bring every thought in every area of life captive to the obedience of Christ (2 Cor. 10:5).

The tools of dominion are given explicit identification in the Scriptures. The Old Testament reveals that faith in the Word of God (Gen. 15:6) and obedience to the law of God are the means of victory for the covenant people (Deut. 4:1-8; 11:13-25; Josh. 1:5-9). The New Testament teaches that the weapons of warfare given to the covenant army of the faithful are not fleshly, but spiritual (2 Cor. 10:3-4). Paul uses the figure of the Roman soldier and the weapons given to him by Rome to conquer the world to identify the spiritual weapons that God has given to Christians to subdue the earth and its rebellion to His kingdom (Eph. 6:11-18). John tells us that the followers of Christ overcome the Serpent and his seed by the power of the redeeming blood of Christ, the Word of God that forms the basis for their testimony, and through an all-out commitment to die, if necessary, for the cause of Christ (Rev. 12:11).

For redeemed man, the Scriptures are the essential tool of dominion. The Bible is the perfect revelation of God to him (Ps. 19:7-13), and it equips him for *every* aspect of his dominion work (2 Tim. 3:15-16).

Conclusion

Scripture says that, "The earth is the Lord's, and fulness thereof; the world, and they that dwell therein" (Ps. 24:1). His ownership and authority is total. Nothing—not even the smallest grain of sand; no creature, man or beast; no institution or realm of man's life—is outside of the dominion of God. Man, as the image of God, shares in this dominion on a creaturely level. That is, God has given man stewardship over the earth to possess it and rule it as His representative and for His glory. Through sin man lost his capacity for godly dominion, but Christ, the God-Man has restored it. Now, in Christ, redeemed man goes forth to take dominion over every part of the earth, every resource of the earth, every creature, every area of life, and every God-ordained institution. The dominion task is necessarily comprehensive, for the earth is the Lord's.

Chapter Six

The Triumph of the Church

From its earliest days and throughout its history, the New Testament church has faced a hostile world intent on its destruction. Today, the church is confronted with enemies on every side, and the persecution of believers is severe in many nations. In the West, the church is no longer respected nor a dominant factor in society; instead, the church is scorned and ridiculed. Evil is on the rise and a pagan worldview has captured the minds of both young and old as the influence of the Christian worldview recedes. Statism has gripped the nations of the world, and men have rejected the Messiah for a messianic state; salvation is seen in terms of government power and legislation, and not in terms of the power of Christ's atoning blood. The laws of God have been set aside for the laws of men. The gospel is preached in many lands and there are many "professions" of faith, but the gospel that is preached is often devoid of a call to repentance and submission to the lordship of Christ. In the majority of churches, the discipleship model is one of pietism, the theology is Arminian and man-centered, and the perspective on the future is pessimistic. As the church enters the 21st century it is in *retreat*, plagued by false doctrine, division, and worldliness. The places where the church is exerting a culture-wide influence are few, if any. The enemies of God are gloating over the fall of the church into irrelevancy and impotency.

Given this sorry state of affairs, there seems to be little room for optimism for the followers of Jesus Christ. The dispensationalists tell us that we are witnessing the inevitable "failure of Christianity" and that the "church age" will end in apostasy in the church and the triumph of evil in the world.[1] John Walvoord states that in this "age of grace . . . things are going to get worse and worse. There will be more oppression, more injustice, more persecution, more immorality as the age wears on."[2] In terms of the future prospects of the church before the end of the age, dispensationalists say that things will actually get worse than they are now. Dispensationalists teach that in history and before the second coming "kingdom power" is withheld from the church, and therefore, the church is "at the mercy of the powers of this world."[3] Hence, the church will not overcome its enemies; rather its enemies shall persecute and nearly crush the church[4] (only a tattered remnant will be rescued by Jesus at the rapture).

But the dispensationalists (and any who hold pessimistic views on the prospects of the church in this age) are seriously mistaken. Yes, the church is in a general state of weakness and decline in our day. However, this condition shall not last, for according to the Scriptures of the Old and New Testaments, *the church of Jesus Christ shall triumph in history and before the second coming.* A brief survey of a few selected texts confirms the glorious future prospects of the church *before* the return of the Lord Jesus Christ at the end of the age.[5]

Old Testament Predictions of Triumph

The significance of the Old Testament for understanding the earthly triumph of the church is based on the New Testament teaching that the church is the new Israel, or "the Israel of God" (Gal. 6:16). The Apostle Paul affirms that believers in Jesus Christ are the true seed of Abraham (Gal. 3:16-17, 26-29), that elect Jews and Gentiles are one body in Christ (Eph. 2:11-3:7), that the

---

[1] For a discussion of the dispensational view of the "church age" and its pessimism concerning it, see William O. Einwechter, "'The Failure of Christianity': The Dispensational View of the Church Age and Its Effect on Christian Political and Social Action," *The Journal of Christian Reconstruction*, vol. xiv, no. 1 (Fall 1996), 223-252.

[2] John F. Walvoord, "Why Must Christ Return?," in *Prophecy in the Seventies*, ed. Charles L. Feinberg (Chicago, 1971), 43.

[3] Robert L. Saucy, "The Presence of the Kingdom and the Life of the Church," *Bibliotheca Sacra* 145 (January - March 1988), 45.

[4] *ibid.*

[5] For a more in-depth study of the scriptural teaching on the triumph of the church in this age see, Kenneth L. Gentry, *He Shall Have Dominion* (Tyler, 1992); Kenneth L. Gentry, *The Greatness of the Great Commission* (Tyler, 1990); Rousas John Rushdoony, *God's Plan for Victory* (Vallecito, [1977] 1997); John J. Davis, *The Victory of Christ's Kingdom* (Moscow, 1996).

Old Testament covenantal distinctions between them have been removed in the church (Eph. 2:11-3:7), and that the New Testament church is the heir of the promises given to Israel (Eph. 2:12, 19-22; 3:6). Hence, the new covenant promises given to Israel are fulfilled in the church (cf. Jer. 31:31-34 with Matt. 26:28; 2 Cor. 3:6; Heb. 8:7-13; 10:12-18). Jesus Christ Himself declared that the kingdom of God would be taken from Israel and given to the church (Matt. 8:10-12; 21:19, 43; Luke 20:9-16). Furthermore, as the new Israel of God, the church is designated by the same terminology that was used in the Old Testament of Israel (cf. 1 Pet. 2:9; Gal. 3:29). Hoekema states: "Is it not abundantly clear . . . that the New Testament church is now the true Israel, in whom and through whom the promises made to Old Testament Israel are being fulfilled?"[6] Therefore, the Old Testament texts that predict the triumph of Israel, Zion, or Judah must be applied to the church, *i.e.,* they predict the triumph of the New Testament church.

1. Genesis 22:17. ". . . and thy seed shall possess the gate of his enemies." This prediction appears in the Lord's word of promise to Abraham in response to his faith and obedience in being willing to follow the Lord's command to sacrifice his only son, Isaac. In context, this prophecy is a part of the comprehensive plan of God for the seed of Abraham: Abraham's seed shall multiply and be as the stars of heaven in number; Abraham's seed will possess the gate of their enemies; Abraham's seed will be the means of blessing to all the nations of the earth (Gen. 22:17-18). Thus, three distinct aspects of the plan of God for Abraham's seed are stated: fantastic growth, triumph over their enemies, and blessing to the nations through them. Carefully note the prediction of triumph. It is as important and distinct as the other two predictions.

The Hebrew word for "possess" *(yarash)* means to take, to take possession of, to inherit, dispossess, or to occupy. The word was commonly used in reference to Israel's possession of the land of Canaan by conquering the inhabitants and occupying their land (Deut. 31:3). The specific object to be possessed in this prediction is the *gate* of their enemies. The word "gate" is filled with significance in the Old Testament. The gate was important for war, commerce, and civil government. In war, if you could breach the gates of a city, victory was nearly assured; control of the gates determined the outcome of the conflict. In commerce, those who controlled the gates determined who could and who could not enter the city to do business. In government, the gate was the place where the elders and rulers of the people would sit to hold court and carry out the other aspects of civil government.

Therefore, to "possess" the gate of your enemy is to conquer him and

---

[6] Anthony A. Hoekema, *The Bible and the Future* (Grand Rapids, 1979), 198.

take control of his city, commerce, and civil government. Genesis 22:17 (cf. also Gen. 24:60) is thus a powerful prediction of the triumph of Jesus Christ and His church (the seed of Abraham) over all of their enemies. In New Testament perspective, it promises the church a comprehensive dominion over the heathen and possession of all the nations of the earth, *i.e.*, all nations will be conquered by the gospel of Christ and be discipled in the Christian faith. Believers in Jesus Christ will dispossess the enemies of God and control the "gate" in all nations.

2. Psalm 110. This Messianic psalm is a declaration of the victorious reign of Christ. This psalm of David predicts the complete triumph of the exalted Christ and His people over the enemies of God. The psalm contains 3 sections: the Messiah's exaltation and promised victorious reign (v. 1); the Messiah's dominion, people, and priesthood (vv. 2-4); and the Messiah's victorious warfare (vv. 5-7). Each section emphasizes Christ's power and His conquest of all who oppose His reign from the Father's right hand.

This psalm is crucial for understanding the fact that the kingdom of Jesus Christ will triumph in history and before the return of Christ. The text establishes that Christ will not leave His place at the Father's right hand in heaven until after all His enemies have become His footstool (v. 1). Christ was exalted to the Father's right hand at the time of His ascension (Acts 2:34-35; Heb. 1:13), and He will not return until the time of the resurrection at the last day when the last enemy, death, will be destroyed (1 Cor. 15:20-28). Therefore, the "day of thy [Christ's] power" (v. 2) when Jesus Christ goes forth to rule and conquer in the midst of His enemies (v. 3) is the *inter-advent period.* The kingdom of Jesus Christ will triumph and all nations will submit to His reign during this age. The return of Christ marks the end of His mediatorial reign (1 Cor. 15:24-25), and the promises of dominion given to Christ in the prophetic Scriptures are fulfilled *before* His second coming.

The church is specifically identified with Christ and His victory in verse 3. The text says, "Thy people will be willing in the day of thy power, in the beauty of holiness from the womb of the morning: thou hast the dew of youth." Here we learn that Christ will not be alone in the conflict, but that He has an army of loyal followers. This army of the Lord is described as being clothed in holy garments and as possessing the strength of youth. During the day of His power (this present age) Christ will be served by a host of willing followers who go with Him into battle. The victorious warfare of the Messiah and His people is described in graphic terminology in verses 5-7. In Revelation 19:11-21, the fulfillment of Psalm 110 is presented to John in a vision of Jesus Christ going forth to conquer His foes. In that vision, as in Psalm 110:3, Christ is followed by an army clothed in holy garments (Rev. 19:14, 19). This army is the church. The church goes forth under Christ, the King, and shall one day share in His victory over all the enemies of God.

3. Isaiah 2:2-4. This prophecy of Isaiah also contains a glorious prediction of the triumph of the church.[7] The passage begins, "And it shall come to pass in the last days, that the mountain of the Lord's house shall be established in the top of the mountains, and shall be exalted above the hills; and all nations shall flow unto it" (v. 2). The "mountain of the Lord's house" is a reference to Zion. In the Old Testament, Zion was often used in a figurative way to refer to God's throne, kingdom, or people. Isaiah uses Zion in a non-literal sense to refer to Yahweh's throne and kingdom (8:18; 33:5, 20; 52:1-2; 24:23; 31:9). He also uses Zion to denote the people of Judah (10:24) and of those who are partakers of the Lord's salvation (12:6; 60:14) and are thus God's covenant people (51:16). In addition, Hebrews 12:22 identifies "mount Sion" as the church of Jesus Christ. Hence, we can conclude that the prophecy of Isaiah concerns the kingdom of God in general, and the church of Jesus Christ in particular. The statement that the mountain of the Lord's house shall be exalted over the mountains and hills indicates the establishment of the sovereign dominion of God's kingdom over all the nations, and the triumph of Christ and His church over all false religions and idolatry.

Furthermore, the text says that "all nations shall flow" unto Zion to be taught the law of God so that they will be able to walk in God's "ways." This is a glorious picture of the nations coming to the church to be taught the Word of God. It foretells the conversion of the nations to the Christian faith. In that day, the church will be the center for the faithful propagation of God's truth for "out of Zion shall go forth the law, and the word of the Lord from Jerusalem" (v.3). And because of the conversion of the nations to the worship and service of Jesus Christ, wars shall cease from the earth (v. 4).

That this prophecy looks forward to the triumph of the church is confirmed by the opening declaration that the exaltation of Zion and the conversion of the nations takes place "in the last days." This phrase is often used in the Old Testament as a technical term to designate the days of the Messiah and His kingdom (Gen. 49:1; Num. 24:14; Dan. 2:28; Hos 3:5; Mic. 4:1-3). The New Testament confirms this usage and explicitly identifies the age between the first and second comings of Christ as the "last days" (cf. Heb. 1:1-2; Acts 2:16-17; 2 Tim. 3:1; James 5:3; 1 Jn. 2:18; 2 Pet. 3:3-4). In the New Testament, the term "last days" does not refer to the days directly preceding Christ's coming or to a future millennial kingdom after Christ returns *but to the entire inter-advent period.* Therefore, all the details of Isaiah 2:2-4 must be fulfilled in and through the New Testament church in this present age.

---

[7] For a detailed discussion of Isa. 2:2-4, see William O. Einwechter, "The Latter Day Triumph of Christ and His Kingdom" *The Journal of Christian Reconstruction,* vol. 15 (Winter, 1998), 107-145.

New Testament Predictions of Triumph

The New Testament not only establishes that the church is the Israel of God and the heir of the Old Testament promises concerning the ascendancy of the covenant people of God over all their enemies, the New Testament also predicts the triumph of the church. Besides the texts that set forth in general terms the invincible nature of Christ and His church,[8] there is also explicit teaching concerning the victory of Christ's kingdom and people.

1. Matthew 28:18-20. The Great Commission is not normally understood as a prediction of the success of the church in converting the nations, but it should be. The plan of the Great Commission is for the church to disciple all nations. It is Christ's will that all peoples and lands be brought to believe in Him and submit to His authority through the Spirit-empowered ministry of the church. The church is to preach the gospel and disciple the converts so that the law of God becomes the law of men and nations. Will Christ's will be fulfilled? Most certainly, for all authority is given to Him in heaven and earth so that He might conquer His enemies and bring all nations under His rule (cf. Ps. 2:8; 110:1-3). Since Christ has all authority in heaven and earth and the church goes forth in His name with His power, who or what can stop the church from fulfilling its task? Christ specifically promises the church His presence to the end of the age so that the church can be assured that it can and will fulfill its divine mission. The Great Commission gives the New Testament perspective on how the Old Testament promises of the conversion of the nations will be fulfilled: they will be fulfilled as the church goes forth in the power of Jesus Christ to preach the gospel and disciple the nations in the law-word of God.

The Great Commission to the church is not the Great Disappointment to the Lord Jesus Christ (which it must be if the church *fails* to disciple the nations). Rather, the Great Commission is the declaration of the sovereign Lord of heaven and earth as to what He intends to accomplish through His people in this age. The Great Commission is a great prediction of the triumph of the church through the power of the risen Christ.[9]

2. Matthew 13:31-43. The parables of the kingdom taught by Jesus during the days of His earthly ministry make certain the triumph of the kingdom of Christ in this age. The parables of the leaven and the mustard seed both indicate that the kingdom of Christ will have a small beginning, but that it shall

---

[8] *cf.* Luke 11:20-22; Col. 2:15; 1 Cor. 15:20-28; Rev. 19:11-16; Matt. 16:18-19; Rom. 8:37; 16:20; 2 Cor. 2:14; 10:3-5; 1 Jn. 5:4.

[9] *cf.* pp. 33-34 of this monograph for further discussion of the Great Commission.

grow to encompass all the earth and all nations. Note that the growth is a continuous process, beginning in the days of Christ and the apostles and continuing until that point in history when all nations shall come under Christ's reign. After Christ ascended to heaven, He sent His Word and Spirit to the church so that it could continue the work that He had begun (cf. Acts 1:1) and be His agent for the fulfillment of the parables of the kingdom. The church, through Christ's power, operates unceasingly through history to leaven the world with the truth of God's Word. The ultimate outcome of the church's ministry is plainly revealed here—all the nations will be converted and enter the kingdom of God in Christ. This is the church's triumph!

The parable of the wheat and tares (Matt. 13:24-32, 36-43) is also a prediction of the worldwide success of the kingdom of Christ. Note, first, that the field is the world and the field belongs to Christ. Second, consider that the "good seed" (believers) is in every part of the field, indicating converts to Christ in every land. Third, understand that at the end of the age the world is not a tare field with a few wheat stalks in it, but a wheat field with some tares present. True, the parable teaches that not every individual will be converted, to Christ, but it also teaches that every nation will be part of the wheat field, *i.e.*, part of Christ's kingdom.

3. Romans 11:11-36. This text outlines the great purpose of God concerning ethnic Israel and the nations during the New Covenant era. First, Israel will remain "blinded in part . . . until the fulness of the Gentiles be come in" (v. 25). Israel will be hardened in unbelief (except for a remnant according to election [Rom. 11:1-7]), until the fulness of Gentiles is accomplished. The phrase "fulness of the Gentiles" speaks of the time when the gospel will have converted the nations to faith in Christ (as predicted in the Old Testament and by Christ). Second, Israel will be provoked to jealousy by the conversion of the nations, and then there will be mass conversions among the Jews and "all Israel will be saved" (vv. 26-27). The Jews will be converted and incorporated into the New Testament church. Third, the result of Israel's conversion will be "the reconciling of the world" and "life from the dead" (v. 15). Both of these phrases speak of the glorious future for the world as all the nations of the world (including Israel) come to faith in Jesus Christ. At that time in history, the world will truly experience "life from the dead," and the great Old Testament prophecies of world-wide blessing through Christ and His church (*e.g.*, Gen. 22:18; Isa. 2:2-4) will come to pass!

Conclusion

The testimony of the Word of God is clear concerning the future triumph of the Lord Jesus Christ and His church. It is hard sometimes to believe that such a glorious future awaits the church. In our day, the church is beset by problems on all sides and is in a state of decline and retreat. Many teach that the best days of the church are behind us, and all that we can expect is the increase of evil and the triumph of wickedness as the age progresses. But don't believe one word of it. The Scriptures declare that the best days for the church still lie in the future; in fact, a most glorious future awaits the followers of Christ! Some have given up, and look only for Christ to rescue them from the present mess (and failure of the church) by the rapture. But don't be like them. Faithfully serve the Lord Jesus Christ because the victory is ours through Him Who loves us. The church—the body of Christ—shall triumph in *His* name over all the enemies of truth and righteousness. Christ is at work in His church at this very hour, laying the foundation for a great resurgence of the Faith. We know this, not by sight, but *by faith* in the Word of God that proclaims the triumph of Christ and His church in the world and in history.

The Author

William O. Einwechter is a teaching elder at Immanuel Free Reformed Church in Ephrata, Pennsylvania, the editor of *The Christian Statesman,* and the vice president of the National Reform Association. He is the author of the books *Ethics and God's Law* and *English Bible Translations*, the editor of the book *Explicitly Christian Politics*, and his essays have appeared in the *Chalcedon Report*, the *Journal of Christian Reconstruction*, *Patriarch,* and *The Christian Statesman.* He holds the Th.M degree from Capital Bible Seminary in Lanham, Maryland. He is an ordained minister and has served in the pastoral ministry since 1982. He and his wife Linda reside with their ten children near Ephrata, Pennsylvania.

The Ministry of Chalcedon

CHALCEDON (kal-see-don) is a Christian educational organization devoted exclusively to research, publishing, and to cogent communication of a distinctly Christian Scholarship to the world at large. It makes available a variety of services and programs, all geared to the needs of interested ministers, scholars, and laymen who understand the proposition that Jesus Christ speaks to the mind as well as to the heart, and that His claims extend beyond the narrow confines of the various institutional churches. We exist in order to support the efforts of all orthodox denominations and churches. Chalcedon derives its name from the great ecclesiastical Council of Chalcedon (A.D. 451), which produced the crucial Christological definition: "Therefore, following the holy Fathers, we all with one accord teach men to acknowledge one and the same Son, our Lord Jesus Christ, at once complete in Godhead and complete in manhood, truly God and truly man. . . ." This formula directly challenges every false claim of divinity by any human institution: state, church, cult, school, or human assembly. Christ alone is both God and man, the unique link between heaven and earth. All human power is therefore derivative: Christ alone can announce that "All power is given unto me in heaven and in earth" (Matthew 28:18). Historically, the Chalcedonian creed is therefore the foundation of Western liberty, for it sets limits on all authoritarian human institutions by acknowledging the validity of the claims of One Who is the source of true human freedom (Galatians 5:1).

The Chalcedon Report is published monthly and is sent to all who request it. All gifts to Chalcedon are tax deductible.

Chalcedon
Box 158
Vallecito, CA 95251 U.S.A.

Books by R. J. Rushdoony

Romans & Galatians

Hebrews, James, & Jude

Institutes of Biblical Law

Law & Society

Systematic Theology

The Politics of Guilt and Pity

Christianity and the State

Salvation and Godly Rule

The Messianic Character of American Education

Roots of Reconstruction

The One and the Many

Revolt Against Maturity

By What Standard?

Law & Liberty

The Biblical Philosophy of History

The Independent Republic

The Nature of the American System

Thy Kingdom Come

For a complete listing of our books contact:

Ross House Books
P.O. Box 67
Vallecito, CA 95251

Grade Three

Acoustic Guitar

Accompaniment

Compiled by

The Specialists in Guitar Education

RGT®

Registry of Guitar Tutors

www.RGT.org

Printed and bound in Great Britain

A CIP record for this publication is available from the British Library
ISBN: 978-1-905908-43-1

Published by Registry Publications

Registry Mews, Wilton Rd, Bexhill, Sussex, TN40 1HY

Text by Tony Skinner and Merv Young.
All musical compositions by Tony Skinner.
Design by JAK Images.
Front cover photo ©Smileus/Fotolia.
Rear cover photo ©ittipol/Fotolia.

Compiled by

www.RGT.org

v.20140214

Contents

Page

CD track listing

Track

1 ▸ Chord Chart 1 – accompaniment demonstration track

2 ▸ Chord Chart 1 – accompaniment practice track

3 ▸ Chord Chart 2 – accompaniment demonstration track

4 ▸ Chord Chart 2 – accompaniment practice track

5 ▸ Chord Chart 3 – accompaniment demonstration track

6 ▸ Chord Chart 3 – accompaniment practice track

7 ▸ Chord Chart 4 – accompaniment demonstration track

8 ▸ Chord Chart 4 – accompaniment practice track

9 ▸ Chord Chart 5 – accompaniment demonstration track

10 ▸ Chord Chart 5 – accompaniment practice track

11 ▸ Chord Chart 6 – accompaniment demonstration track

12 ▸ Chord Chart 6 – accompaniment practice track

13 ▸ Chord Chart 7 – accompaniment demonstration track

14 ▸ Chord Chart 7 – accompaniment practice track

15 ▸ Chord Chart 8 – accompaniment demonstration track

16 ▸ Chord Chart 8 – accompaniment practice track

17 ▸ Chord Chart 9 – accompaniment demonstration track

18 ▸ Chord Chart 9 – accompaniment practice track

19 ▸ Chord Chart 10 – accompaniment demonstration track

20 ▸ Chord Chart 10 – accompaniment practice track

Introduction

This book is designed primarily to provide supplementary learning materials for candidates preparing for the Accompaniment section of the Registry of Guitar Tutors (RGT) Grade Three acoustic guitar playing exam. However, it should also prove helpful for anyone wishing to improve their accompaniment skills.

Accompaniment is an important skill for any guitarist and is particularly relevant for acoustic guitarists who might be accompanying someone singing (be it themselves or another vocalist) or accompanying another instrumentalist.

In essence, the role of an accompanist is to bring two elements to the overall performance: rhythm and harmony. The chords themselves provide the harmony and the timing of how the chords are played provides the rhythm. In this book the focus is predominantly on the rhythmic elements, as this is where the main decisions are to be made at this level of playing. You will, however, find fretboxes, showing the recommended fingering, for all the new chords required at this level on page 20 in the Chord Shapes chapter.

This book contains 10 melodies, that have been notated, along with the appropriate chord chart for each one. There are also some tips with each example to get you thinking about how to approach developing your own rhythm playing ideas.

There is also a CD with this book that contains each melody being played on two different tracks. The first CD track for each melody features a guitar playing an example chord accompaniment along with the melody (played twice). The second CD track features the melody on its own (played three times), so that you can play the chords and practise your own accompaniment skills.

The CD demo recordings that are provided with this book are intended to give an indication of the technical level that would be expected for a high mark at this grade. To ensure that you can hear the accompaniment guitar part on the CD demo tracks clearly, the level of the accompaniment guitar has deliberately been made louder than might normally occur in a standard recording. The demo recordings of the accompaniment parts are not intended to provide exact templates for candidates to copy; they are provided as examples of the standard required, and candidates are strongly encouraged to devise their own rhythmic/picking styles.

The demo recordings also provide an insight into the factors that need to be considered when developing accompaniment ideas. When accompanying, each melody can be interpreted in a number of ways and there will be a range of playing techniques and rhythm styles that can be effectively adopted. The aim of this book is to enable the player to start developing their playing skills so that sympathetic musical decisions can be made to both support and enhance the melody being played.

Exam Format

In the accompaniment section of the RGT acoustic guitar exams, the candidate is required to play a chordal accompaniment while the examiner plays an eight-bar melody.

In the exam, the candidate will be shown a chord chart for the melody. The examiner will then give a one bar count-in and play the melody once, just for the candidate to listen to without playing along. The examiner will then give another one bar count-in and the melody will be played a further three times without stopping. The candidate can accompany the first of these three verses if they wish to, but only the accompaniment of the second and third verses will be assessed.

The style of the accompaniment is left to the candidate's discretion, and the candidate can chose to either strum or fingerpick.

At this grade, the chord charts will be in either $^{3}{}_{4}$ or $^{4}{}_{4}$ time. There will be seven *different* chords in each chord chart, one of which will last for two bars; the other chords will last for one bar each. In the very final bar (after the repeat) the chord should be played with a single strum.

The range of chords that may occur at this grade are listed in the Chord Charts chapter of this book.

The examiner will play the melody either live on a guitar or keyboard, or via a recording. The melody notation played by the examiner will not be seen by the candidate. This way the candidate can focus on the chord chart and using their musical and aural abilities to create the most appropriate accompaniment.

The examiner will 'cue you in' when you are due to start playing the accompaniment (the method of doing so may vary according to the melody being played). As part of your practice with this book, work on being able to follow the chord charts so that you know exactly when to come in by yourself.

At this grade it is expected that candidates will include some rhythmic and dynamic variation in their playing.

As the main purpose of this section of the exam is to assess the candidate's ability to make musical decisions about the most appropriate way to perform the chords that are presented, the examiner will not provide any advice on how to play the accompaniment.

Accompaniment Advice

Your playing should always relate to the timing and style of the melody played by the examiner. Remember that the very first time the examiner plays the melody, you have the opportunity to listen to it without needing to play along. Use this opportunity to listen carefully and try to absorb the melodic shape and structure of the melody. During the first (unassessed) accompaniment verse it may be best if you just strum a chord once on the first beat of each bar, so that you can get a feel for the timing of the piece. However, if you prefer, another approach would be just to read through the chord chart and listen as the examiner plays the first verse of the melody. When you are preparing for this section of the exam, in advance of the exam date, try out both approaches to see which one is more effective for you. Whichever method you adopt, do make sure you are following the chord chart carefully so that you are ready to start your accompaniment once the melody commences for the second verse.

In the remaining two verses use an appropriate rhythm or picking style that suits the mood, style and timing of the melody. When you are practising the examples in this book, keep experimenting to develop your own musical ideas. Listen out for any prominent rhythmic elements of the melody that you can respond to and emulate with the chords. Alternatively, if there is a bar with only a few melody notes, you might choose to play a busier rhythm in this bar to create a musical contrast.

Keep listening closely to the melody while playing your accompaniment and make sure to keep in time with it. Practise carefully to ensure that your chords come in on the first beat of each bar, to help establish a definite pulse and rhythm.

Ensure that you are totally comfortable with playing all the chord shapes on their own before you attempt them with the accompaniment practice track. There are several new chords introduced at this grade, some of which may prove tricky at first, so practise these carefully and separately. In order to ensure that the chords sound clearly, make sure that your fretting fingers are as close to the frets as they can be.

Use your knowledge of the chord shapes to change smoothly from one chord to another, whilst making sure your chords ring clear. It might be that the strumming is fluent but the chord changes are not as smooth as they need to be. In that case, initially try playing along with one of the example melodies but just strumming each chord once – to give yourself more time to change onto the next chord. (Remember that this advice is only for practising the chord changes, not how to play in the exam itself.) As this becomes comfortable, try strumming each chord twice and build up from there until you have the confidence to play the full strumming pattern.

Take time to listen to how the chords themselves sound. It is very easy to get too wrapped up in the fingering and chord shapes and not listen carefully to the actual sound being produced. Are all the strings ringing out clearly? Is there buzzing from any of the fretted notes?

Use Some Variations

At this level it's important to include some variation of your rhythm pattern in the final verse. Think about ways to develop your original strumming pattern ideas as you are playing with the practice tracks. See if you can incorporate some variations as you are playing along and listen out for points where some variation will be particularly effective, for instance, in the final bar before the progression repeats. If this doesn't work at first, try your ideas on their own, without the practice track, and then have another go. The more you practise this, the more instinctive this ability will become.

$^3{}_4$ Time Signature

At this grade, as well as $^4{}_4$ time, the chord chart may be in $^3{}_4$ time. If the $^3{}_4$ time signature is new to you, then keep your rhythms and strumming very simple to start with – try just strumming or plucking the chord three times evenly in each bar; don't try to vary from this until playing in this time signature feels totally comfortable. When you are ready to try incorporating some upstrokes or other variations to develop this basic pattern, be careful not to make the pattern too busy – as $^3{}_4$ time often occurs in a ballad or other relaxed musical style.

Use Some Dynamics

On several of the CD demonstration tracks you'll hear that some 'dynamic variation' (changes of volume when playing) has been used to add interest and contrast to the performance. Listen carefully to how changing the strength of strumming (and therefore the volume) has been used to create some excitement or emotion in the rhythm playing that empathises with the melody line. Experiment with varying from loud to soft playing (or vice-versa) during your own practice, so that you can then incorporate some of this technique into your accompaniment playing, when musically appropriate. Be aware that a common mistake when first using dynamics is to speed up slightly when starting to strum louder and to slow down a little as you try to play more softly; listen out for this against the timing of the melody you are playing with and keep practising until you can stay in time whilst changing volume.

Keep Playing

If you make a mistake whilst playing the accompaniment, DO NOT STOP. It is important for the overall musical result that you keep playing (something – anything!) so that you do not lose your place in the music and fall out of time with the melody. Regardless of what mistake you might make with a chord shape, it will never sound worse than if you come to a complete halt – particularly as the melody will carry on without you. If you cannot change to a chord in time, then simply place your fretting hand across the strings to mute them whilst you carry on strumming – it's not ideal, but it will definitely sound preferable to a total halt and the risk of losing your co-ordination with the melody.

Chord Charts

Examples of the type of chord charts that will occur in the Accompaniment section of the Grade Three RGT acoustic guitar playing exam are given on the following pages. Note that these chord charts are provided only as examples of *the types* of chord charts that may occur in the exam.

The new chords that may occur at this grade are:

Asus2 Dsus2 Fsus2 Asus4 Csus4 Dsus4 Esus4 Fsus4 Gsus4

Fretboxes showing the suggested fingering for these chords are provided at the back of this book. You do not have to use the same fingering as shown in this book or in the exam handbook; any alternative chord fingerings will be acceptable, provided the chords are musically correct.

In addition, the chords from previous grades may also occur in the chord charts for this grade:

A C D E F G Am Dm Em A7 B7 C7 D7 E7 G7
Amaj7 Cmaj7 Dmaj7 Fmaj7 Gmaj7 Am7 Dm7 Em7

Please study the earlier books in this series if you are not familiar with any of these lower grade chords.

Below each example chord chart in this chapter, the melody, that it is designed to accompany, is provided in both standard notation and tablature. Note that in the exam itself, the melody will NOT be shown to the candidate; it is provided in this book purely for situations where a teacher might wish to play the melody with a student rather than use the CD provided.

A sample rhythm pattern has been notated below each chord chart in this chapter; this is the main rhythm pattern that is used on the demonstration track. However, at this grade, candidates are not expected to limit their playing to exactly the same rhythm in every bar, hence many variations (from subtle additions to and omissions from the notated rhythm, as well as more obvious contrasts) are included in the demonstration track performances. The demonstration tracks provide examples of the standard required for a high mark at this grade. Each rhythm pattern has been designed to reflect some of the main rhythmic features of the melody. The rhythm pattern can be used as a starting point for your own rhythm playing. However, for each chord chart, this will be just one of many different interpretations that are possible and you are encouraged to explore and practise different rhythm patterns so as to develop your accompaniment skill and your ability to reflect the main rhythmic elements of a melody. Note that, on the CD, only the last two verses are provided on the demonstration track recording for each chord chart.

For each example on the following pages there are some specific tips and advice that are relevant to that chord chart and melody. Use these as ideas from which to start developing your own interpretations. The advice is intended to help you to develop your own skills and confidence in this area of playing.

Chord Chart 1 (CD Track 1)

On the demonstration track the following rhythm pattern is used *as the basis* for the chord playing:

The melody for this example has a fairly relaxed feel in $^3{}_4$ time. On the demonstration track the eighth note that occurs after beat 2 is played with an upstroke to help emphasise this relaxed nature and the chords are generally strummed with quite a light feel. This rhythm pattern reflects the melody that is played in bars 1 and 3, but also acts as a contrast to the melody in the remaining bars.

On the demonstration track a simple variation is played in bars 4 and 8 during the first verse, with further developments being played in the second verse. For instance, a busier strumming pattern is adopted in bars 2, 4, 7 and 8 in the second verse to act as a contrast to the simpler rhythm of the melody that occurs in these bars.

Melody 1 (CD Track 2)

Chord Chart 2 (CD Track 3)

| 4/4 ‖: D | Dsus2 | G | Gmaj7 |

| Em | Em7 | A | A :‖ D |

On the demonstration track the following rhythm pattern is used *as the basis* for the chord playing:

The melody has quite a sparse feel to it so, to act as a contrast, a slightly busier rhythm pattern has been used. On the demonstration track you'll also hear that bars 7 and 8 of the first verse are played with a slightly busier rhythm that provides some drive and momentum towards the second verse, where more variations are used throughout. More use of eighth notes is made during the second verse, although predominantly with the same combination of downstrokes and upstrokes to maintain a relaxed feel. However, in bar 8 the strumming switches to mainly downstrokes playing eighth notes to create some additional energy prior to the final chord ending.

As well as the variations outlined above, you'll also notice that this demonstration track (and many others) features some subtle variations to the rhythm pattern through the use of 'ghost strums'. This is where a chord is only partially sounded or strummed; the technique helps maintain the momentum of the rhythm and generates additional interest by not rigidly following a repetitive rhythm.

Melody 2 (CD Track 4)

Chord Chart 3 (CD Track 5)

$\frac{3}{4}$ |: F | Fsus2 | Csus4 | C |

Am7 | Am7 | Dm7 | C7 :|| F ||

On the demonstration track the following rhythm pattern is used *as the basis* for the chord playing:

The melody has a relaxed feel in $^3_4$ time, with the rhythm of the second half of the melody (in bars 5 to 8) being different from the first four bars. To reflect this, a different playing approach has been adopted for those chords on the demonstration track.

During the first few bars the chords are 'broken' by picking the lower (bass) notes of the chord followed by strumming the higher strings. In the rhythm pattern notated above, the two eighth notes are the individual notes that are picked first. Thereafter the chords are strummed using this pattern as the basis for the rhythm. You will hear that the second verse in particular features some busier variations to this strumming pattern, such as in bars 4 and 7.

All the time quite a light and relaxed feel has been maintained, even during the strumming variations. When developing your own rhythm ideas always consider an appropriate style of playing so that your playing works well with the melody.

Melody 3 (CD Track 6)

Chord Chart 4 (CD Track 7)

| 4/4 ||: G | G | Dsus4 | D |

| Am | Em | Am7 | Cmaj7 :|| G

On the demonstration track the following rhythm pattern is used *as the basis* for the chord playing:

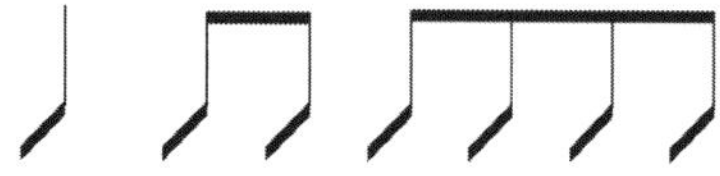

This rhythm pattern reflects some of the features of the melody, for instance the eighth notes that occur in bars 2 and 6. However, it also then acts as a contrast to the simpler melody notes in the remaining bars.

On the demonstration track the rhythm is played using a combination of downstrokes and upstrokes, although how these are used varies throughout both verses. Varying the direction of the strumming can be a very effective device to generate interest and energy throughout a performance, so listen to the track carefully to gauge the impact. For instance, bars 3 and 4 of the second verse are played with mainly downstrokes – this helps to create a dynamic build in the music, and is followed by a more relaxed feel as the second verse comes to a close. The final two bars are played lightly with downstrokes and upstrokes prior to gently strumming the final chord. Experiment with how you can use different strumming techniques to vary the dynamics of your playing to effectively complement the melody.

Melody 4 (CD Track 8)

hord Chart 5 (CD Track 9)

4/4 ‖: Am7 | Am7 | Dm7 | Fmaj7 |

Gsus4 | G | Em | Dm :‖ Am7 ‖

On the demonstration track the rhythm pattern varies to reflect the melody itself. For nstance the following pattern is used as the basis for the first three bars:

You'll also hear the following rhythm adopted in places during bars 5 to 8 to reflect the melody played during some of those bars:

The approach here is not to copy exactly the rhythm of the melody, but rather to draw on some of the characteristic elements and reflect these. As you are experimenting with your own ideas listen carefully for any obvious aspects of the melody that you can draw on and develop.

You'll hear on the demonstration track that the rhythm patterns are played using a combination of downstrokes and upstrokes to maintain a fairly light and relaxed feel throughout.

Melody 5 (CD Track 10)

Chord Chart 6 (CD Track 11)

4/4 ‖: Dm	Fsus2	C	Csus4

Am	Am7	A7	A7	:‖ Dm

On the demonstration track the following syncopated rhythm pattern (1 2&[3]&4) is used *as the basis* for the chord playing during the first verse:

This strumming pattern is played using downstrokes and upstrokes (Down DownUp UpDown) and reflects some of the rhythmic elements of the melody.

During the second verse the performance is given a lift by adopting a different strumming technique. The chords are played with eighth notes throughout, however, the chords played on beats 2 and 4 are damped to create the percussive sound you can hear on the demonstration track. This is accomplished by placing the side of your strumming hand against the strings of the guitar and simultaneously strumming down quite firmly to create a percussive 'click' sound across the strings. This technique can be a little tricky at first, so practise it with a single chord before you try to change chords or play the whole progression. Percussive devices such as these can be a highly effective method of generating extra momentum and energy, so persevere with this technique and experiment with it further.

Melody 6 (CD Track 12)

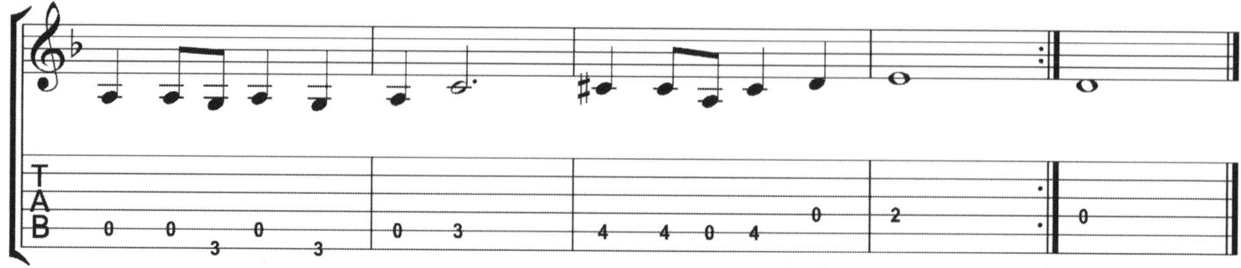

hord Chart 7 (CD Track 13)

| $\frac{3}{4}$ ||: Em | D | Cmaj7 | B7 |

| Am | Am | Dsus4 | D7 | :|| Em ||

n the demonstration track the chords are played with the following rhythm pattern 1 most of the bars:

he melody here is in $^3{}_4$ time, and this straightforward rhythm has been adopted to ighlight the essence of this time signature. The musical interest is created by how he chords are being played: with the bass note of each chord being picked with the humb on the first beat of the bar, three fingers are then used to gently 'pluck' the op three strings of each chord on beats 2 and 3.

During the second verse you'll hear that the plucking rhythm is different in bars 3 nd 7, where the exact rhythm of the melody is copied to create a sense of novement here.

lthough thumb and fingers were used on the demonstration track, the bass notes ould also be played using a pick (plectrum) instead of the thumb. The remaining hord notes could then either be plucked with the fingers, as described above, or trummed using a pick. Experiment to find a method that feels the most comfortable or you. Keep your approach light and relaxed though, especially when plucking the igher strings.

Melody 7 (CD Track 14)

Chord Chart 8 (CD Track 15)

| 4/4 |: A | Asus2 | D | Dsus2 |

| E | E | Dmaj7 | E7 :| A |

On the demonstration track the chords are played with the following rhythm patter in several places throughout both verses:

The small arrow heads underneath some of the notes are 'accent' marks, whic mean the chords should be emphasised more on these beats. On the demonstratio track this is accomplished by playing the strumming pattern using 'palm mutin with the picking hand. In order to palm mute you place the heel of your pick han gently against the bass guitar strings on or near the bridge and then strum th strings. To create the accented notes the chords on these beats are played *withou* palm muting, i.e. by removing the muting hand slightly away from the strings so tha they sound more clearly. Take care to ensure all the notes sound clearly whe playing the accented chord by making sure you strum all the required strings. If thi is a new technique to you, try getting used to playing the chords with palm mutin throughout at first, before you attempt to switch between the two different playin techniques.

You'll hear on the demonstration track that the position and duration of thes accents varies in places and some bars contain more or less palm muted notes tha others. For instance, bars 7 and 8 in the second verse are played with no pal muting at all to create some extra energy before the final chord.

Melody 8 (CD Track 16)

Chord Chart 9 (CD Track 17)

3/4 |: Amaj7 | Amaj7 | D | Dmaj7 |

Esus4 | E | Asus4 | E7 :| Amaj7 ||

On the demonstration track the chords are played using a fingerstyle pattern rather than being strummed:

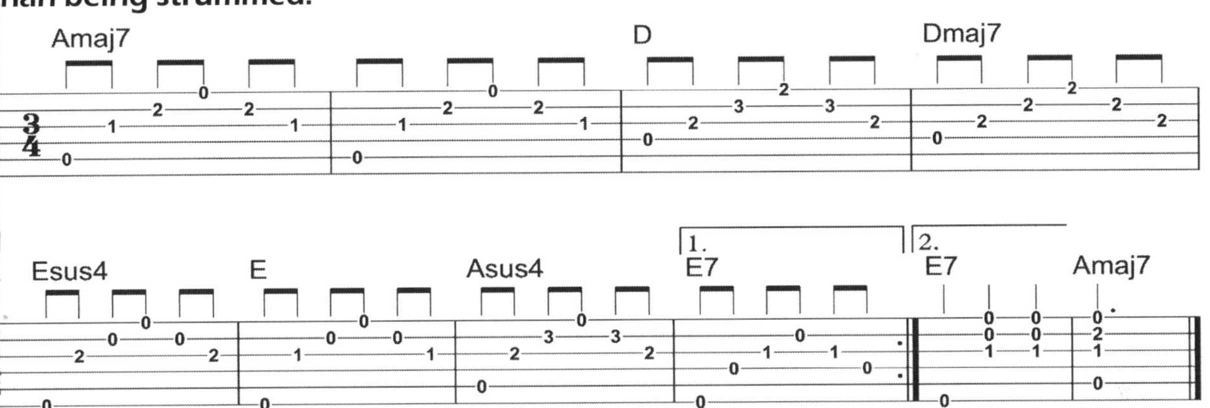

This features a steady eighth note pattern that serves as a smooth foundation for the melody itself. On the demonstration track the bass note of each chord is picked using the thumb, followed by the remaining notes being picked by fingers 12321. This style of pattern can also be produced effectively by using a pick (plectrum) to play each individual note. In the penultimate bar prior to the final chord you'll notice that the three high strings are played together by gently plucking simultaneously with fingers 1, 2 and 3. Notice how there is some dynamic contrast in the second verse, with the chords being played a little louder towards the end. Practise using dynamics to help develop your technical control with this style of playing, so you'll then be able to use dynamic contrasts in your accompaniments whenever you feel they'll be appropriate and aid the musical result.

Melody 9 (CD Track 18)

Chord Chart 10 (CD Track 19)

| 4/4 |: F | Fsus4 | Fsus2 | Dm7 |

| C | Am | Dm | Dm :| F |

On the demonstration track the following rhythm pattern (1&2&[3]&4) has been adopted *as the basis* of the performance:

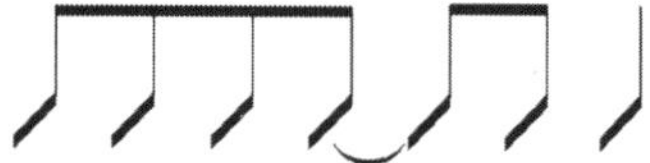

During the first four bars in both verses the chords on beats 2 and 4 are damped to create a percussive sound (as described in the text for Chord Chart 6). The second half of verse 1 uses the same rhythm pattern but the chords are played without this damped technique, to act as a contrast and to create extra interest.

In bars 6, 7 and 8 of the second verse, the chords are quickly picked through from the bass notes to the high notes to create an arpeggiated feel. Listen to the demonstration track carefully to hear the effect this creates prior to the final chord being played.

Melody 10 (CD Track 20)

Chord Shapes

The next page provides the fingering for the new chords that are introduced in the Accompaniment section of the Grade Three RGT acoustic guitar playing exam.

f, in the exam, you prefer to use an alternative fingering for any chord, that would be perfectly acceptable, providing the pitches are all accurate and an effective musical result is produced.

n addition to the chords shown overleaf, you will need to know the following chords from lower grades. Please consult the earlier books in this series if you are unsure about any of these chords.

Minor chords:

Am Dm Em

Major chords:

A C D E F G

Minor 7 chords:

Am7 Dm7 Em7

Dominant 7 chords:

A7 B7 C7 D7 E7 G7

Major 7 chords:

Amaj7 Cmaj7 Dmaj7 Fmaj7 Gmaj7

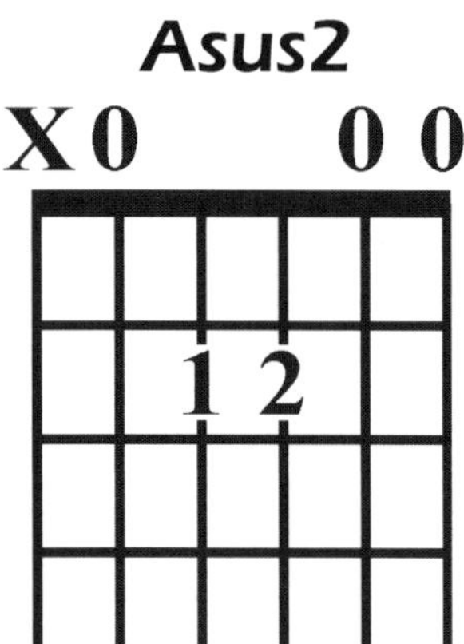
Asus2
X 0 0 0
1 2

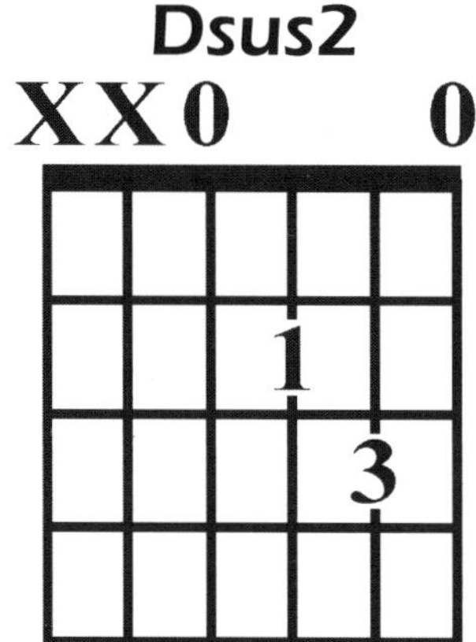
Dsus2
X X 0 0
1
3

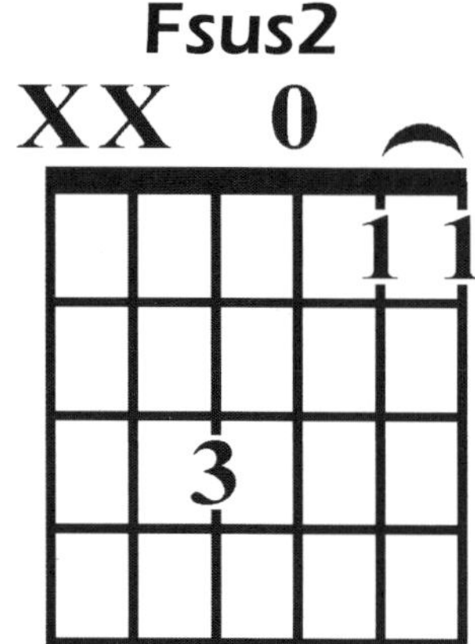
Fsus2
X X 0
1 1
3

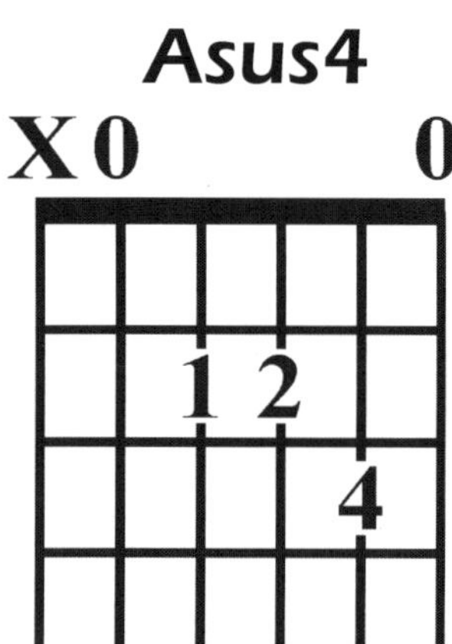
Asus4
X 0 0
1 2
4

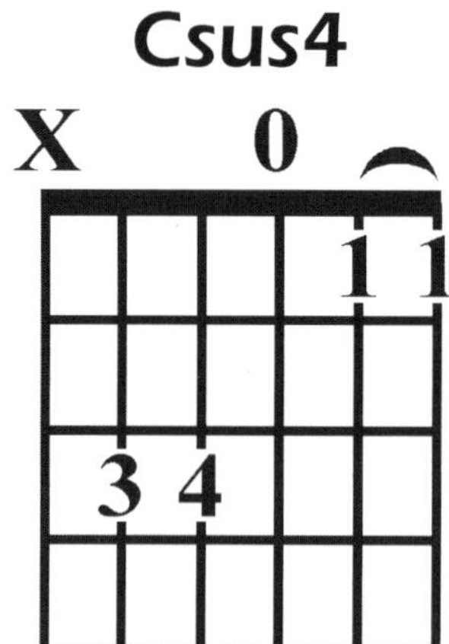
Csus4
X 0
1 1
3 4

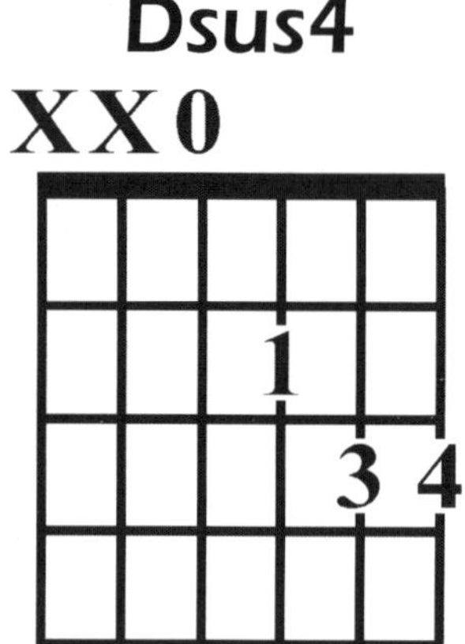
Dsus4
X X 0
1
3 4

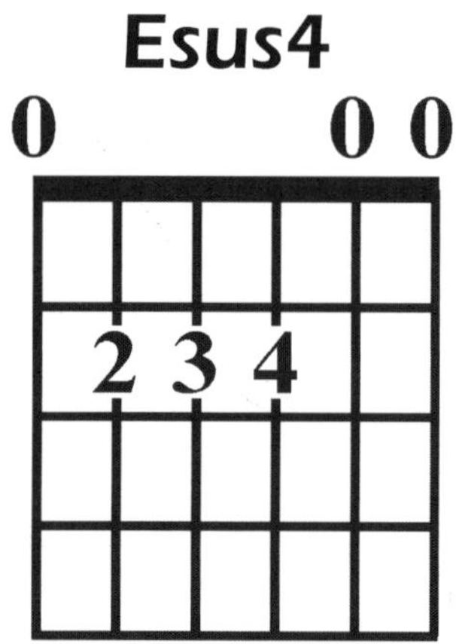
Esus4
0 0 0
2 3 4

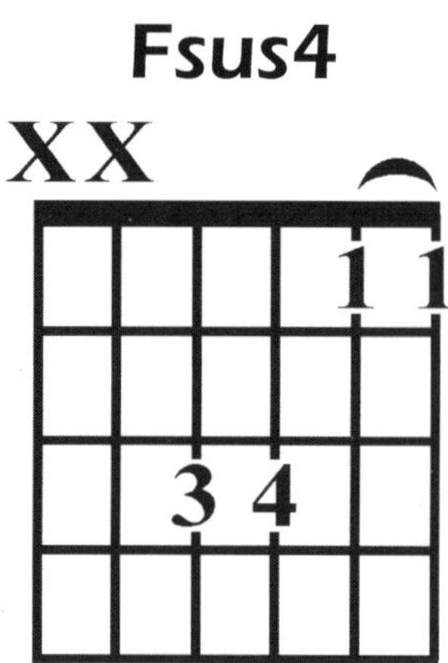
Fsus4
X X
1 1
3 4

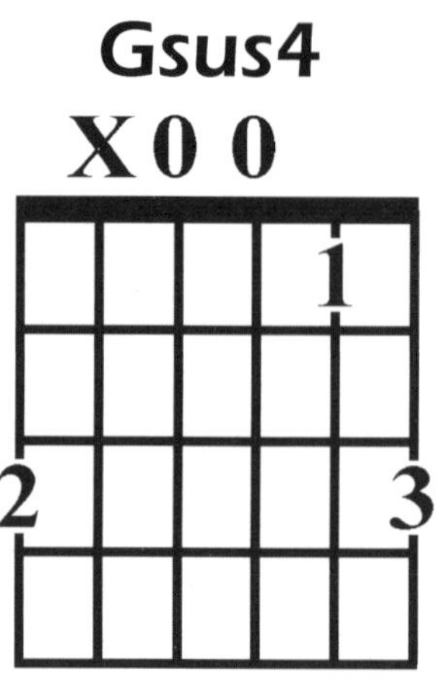
Gsus4
X 0 0
1
2 3